Also by Tom Bullough

FICTION

A

The Claude Glass

Konstantin

Addlands

SARN HELEN

A Journey Through Wales, Past, Present and Future

TOM BULLOUGH

With illustrations by Jackie Morris

GRANTA

Granta Publications, 12 Addison Avenue, London W11 4QR
First published in Great Britain by Granta Books, 2023

'Prayer of Penitence' from *A Time for Creation* is copyright
© The Archbishops' Council, 2020. Published by Canterbury Press.
Used by permission. rights@hymnsam.co.uk

A CIP catalogue record for this book
is available from the British Library.

3 5 7 9 10 8 6 4 2

ISBN 978 1 78378 809 5
eISBN 978 1 78378 810 1

www.granta.com

Map by John Gilkes

Typeset in Minion by M Rules

Printed and bound in Great Britain by T J Books, Padstow

For Alice and Edwyn

Contents

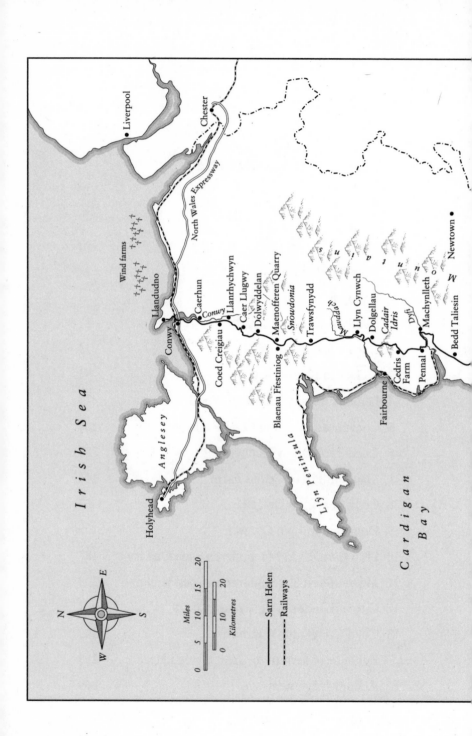

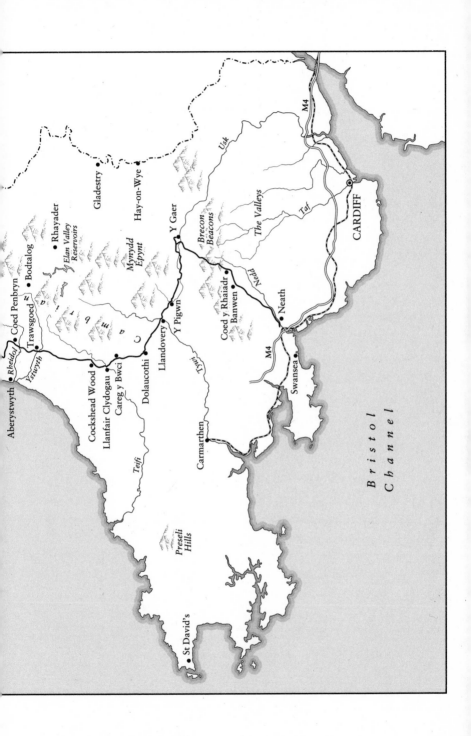

Note on illustrations

As I write – and Jackie paints – the most recent *State of Nature* report was published in 2019. According to this, of 3,902 species assessed, seventy-three have disappeared from Wales over the past fifty years. A further 666 species – 17 per cent – are threatened with imminent national extinction.

These illustrations show fifteen of those species, plus (last in the list) one now considered extinct:

- kestrel (p. 2)
- orca (p. 8)
- spreading bellflower (p. 30)
- otter (p. 50)
- pearl-bordered fritillary (p. 76)
- sand lizard (p. 100)
- Bechstein's bat (p. 120)
- puffin (p. 138)
- red squirrel (p. 154)
- cuckoo (p. 172)
- narrow-bordered bee hawk-moth (p. 184)
- Menai whitebeam (p. 202)
- water vole (p. 228)
- large mason bee (p. 246)
- eel (p. 256)
- turtle dove (p. 266)

SARN
HELEN

Prologue

It must have been ten years ago or more when it struck me that I had to walk Sarn Helen: the Roman road which once ran from Neath, almost on the south coast of Wales, all the way to Caerhun, almost on the north. At the time this was plainly impossible. I had recently become a father; a trip to the shop seemed the height of ambition. All the same, the idea would not go away – and not only because the road bisects the hill behind our house in the Brecon Beacons. Wales is a small, fragmented country, divided by language, landscape and tradition. Of those things that bind it together, Sarn Helen is surely the earliest: a first, great piece of infrastructure. True, most of the original road is gone, along with its forts, its ports and its mines. But that it is now almost an arbitrary line, a cross-section of farms and hillsides, obscure villages and post-industrial towns – this only added to its allure.

In the end it was not until summer 2020, not long after the first Covid-19 lockdown, that I took a bus from Llanspyddid to Neath – wandering down the Swansea Valley, through Abercrâf and Ystradgynlais, while the other passengers, muffled by their face masks, exchanged greetings of long, soft vowels. Even then my plan was just to walk for two days, back across the Beacons to Y Gaer, the Roman fort at the bottom of our hill. Certainly I had no thoughts of writing about it. The fact was, as for so many others, that these had been four months of relentless childcare, mostly in a confined space. All I wanted was air and quiet and a landscape I didn't know inside out.

The experience changed that, almost at once. Wales is my home, in every sense, but I grew up on a hill farm in Radnorshire, Powys; I come from the border parts of the country: an area of divided identity, which has, in many ways, defined my life. For years, to bring some peace to my relationship with Wales, I have immersed myself in its history and legend, its culture, ecology and languages. What I found, as I tramped out of Neath and on to a long, straight track heading north, was that everything I met was informed by this knowledge – that the road, in fact, was the perfect spine from which to flesh out a picture of the country: Wales present and Wales past. Not that this would be a regular history of the birth of Wales in the ruins of the Roman Empire, of its conquest by England in the thirteenth century, of the coming of devolution in the 1990s. Rather, it would be an exploration of its origins – of that post-Roman period, the 'Age of Saints', dating roughly from AD 450 to 700. Particularly, I wanted to consider what these saints – these ancient holy men and women who, as heirs both to Christian and Celtic traditions, perceived the divine in the landscape of Wales – might bring to our relationship with the natural world.

This, after all, is the issue of our times.

All of which meant that, out of necessity, it would also be a book about Wales future: a future which, since globally we are conducting a chemical experiment – introducing, for one thing, about 36 billion tonnes of carbon dioxide into the atmosphere every year – can in certain respects be reliably predicted. In such stages as life would allow I continued north along Sarn Helen. I walked from Y Gaer to Llandovery. I walked from Llandovery to Machynlleth. And, meanwhile, I began to speak to experts – to check if my understanding of climate and ecology could really be accurate, to weave these conversations into the text. In sum, I thought, past, present and future might give some sense of the stakes, of what Wales stands to lose. Not because the country is in any way the front line in the climate and ecological emergency. Not because its predicament is even remarkable – except to those of us for whom it is home, for whom it means our children's lives. More because we face a threat so inconceivably vast that, really, it is only on a very small scale that it can seem to mean anything at all.

Wales, in the UK at least, is often employed as a unit of measurement. Turn your attention to the BBC News and the chances are that, soon enough, you will learn that an iceberg is 'quarter of the size of Wales' or that the wetlands of South Sudan are 'two times the size of Wales'. As a key to imagining magnitudes, from meteorite strikes to the Amazon rainforest (of which an area half the size of Wales was lost between August 2020 and July 2021), it is clearly felt small enough to be comprehensible. Perhaps, I thought, it might function as a key here too. Perhaps a glimpse into the future of Wales could give a glimpse into the future of us all – and, in doing so, provide some sense of the ways in which we must respond.

Llanspyddid, July 2022

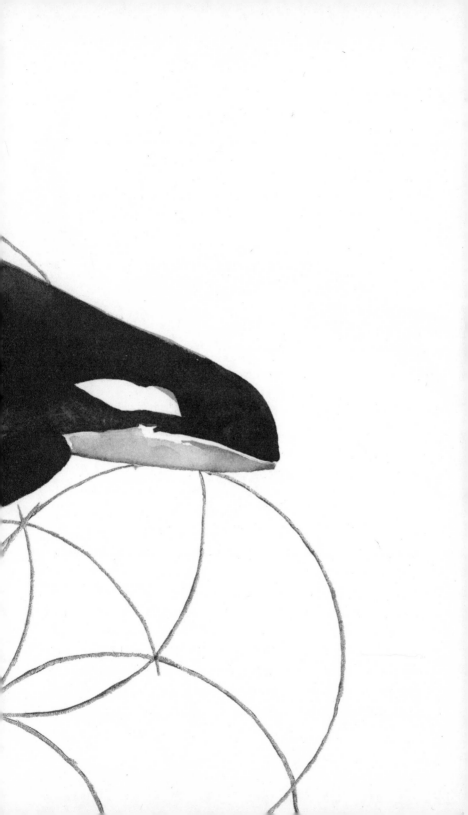

I

Neath to Coed y Rhaiadr

29 July 2020

Here, in this square of rusty railings, are an Oranjeboom can, a Walkers packet, a birthday card of a year or more's vintage and a couple of groups of dressed stone foundations. Also, as if pressed to the bars, a copper-green plaque reading: 'ROMAN NEATH (NIDUM). SOUTH GATE OF FORT'. To the one side is Neath Abbey Road: sporadic cars and distanced pedestrians, plane trees lining the playing fields of Dŵr-y-Felin Comprehensive School. To the other are the houses of Roman Way, whose roofs appear to have overflowed so that tiles surround the first-floor windows. Their garden walls resemble the foundations. Behind one, a man is digging; there is little to see but the top of his head, which is freshly shaved and mirrors the clouds. He has bags of cement, a coil of pipe and a growing pile of earth and rubble.

'Does it mean anything much to you,' I ask, 'that this used to be a Roman fort?'

'Well.' He rests, joins his hands on his spade. 'I tell you what, it does help the digging. I could use a pot of gold just now.'

'To be honest with you,' says a woman on the pavement, 'I know nothing whatsoever about it.' She is slight with sandy-grey hair, sandy-grey clothes and a lively face, a ruddiness waiting just under the skin. The weight of her voice lands fully on the vowels. She laughs. 'I should find out, really, shouldn't I? I mean, here's me, right the way through lockdown . . . Time was, when I wanted a walk, I'd always pop on the bus to Swansea Beach. These past few months, I've found out everything local. There's waterfalls just by there, up the Clydach. I never knew that. I've walked up the Dulais. I've walked to Resolven. And all along I'm living in a Roman fort!'

She roots in her handbag, finds a cigarette.

'You'll be headed up Cadoxton,' she says. 'Well, you shall have to see the Murder Stone. By the path in the churchyard, it is. Great big thing. You cannot miss it . . .'

It can often be like this, in South Wales towns. You speak to somebody; they reply, in the way of probably knowing your mother. Once, when I was working at my father's sawmill, on the Wales–England border near Hay-on-Wye, a lorry driver phoned up, wild, in tears. A young man from the Rhondda, he had travelled to London and set about knocking on people's doors to get some help in unloading his floorboards. He had never been to London before. The fear he was met with, the universal rejection, he found so entirely overwhelming that a carpenter had to be scrambled from Richmond to explain that this was not suburban Glamorgan, that you could not expect the entire street to come and get involved.

Suburban Glamorgan. The new-mown grass. The occasional conservatory. The universal tributes to the NHS. Cadoxton Road may not be pretty with its culs-de-sac of modern houses traced by the rush of the A465, the pungent Nedd and the Tennant Canal in its skin of dank weeds, but all the same it has a geniality, a sense that here it is possible to breathe. A brow of oak and sycamore gathers, rears over roofs and red-dragon flags. At one of the junctions a man in an Audi lifts a thumb, gestures for me to cross before him – past Les Davies, Funeral Director, into the churchyard of St Catwg's Church.

On a bench, his jeans too tight for his heft, a boy is cackling into a phone.

The Murder Stone would, indeed, be difficult to miss. Six feet tall, in the shape of an obelisk, it stands against a mass of bindweed and couch grass, bellowing in deep-carved capitals:

1823/ TO RECORD/ MURDER/ THIS STONE
WAS ERECTED/ OVER THE BODY OF/
MARGARET WILLIAMS/ AGED 26/ A NATIVE
OF CARMARTHENSHIRE/ LIVING IN SERVICE
IN THIS PARISH/ WHO WAS FOUND DEAD/
WITH MARKS OF VIOLENCE UPON HER
PERSON/ IN A DITCH ON THE MARSH/ BELOW
THIS CHURCHYARD/ ON THE MORNING OF
SUNDAY THE FOURTEENTH OF JULY/ 1822

ALTHOUGH/ THE SAVAGE MURDERER/
ESCAPE FOR A SEASON THE DETECTION
OF MAN/ YET/ GOD HATH SET HIS
MARK UPON HIM/ EITHER FOR TIME OR
ETERNITY/ AND/ THE CRY OF BLOOD/ WILL
ASSUREDLY PURSUE HIM/ TO CERTAIN
AND TERRIBLE RIGHTEOUS/ JUDGMENT

According to the woman back on Roman Way, the people of Cadoxton were so horrified that such a crime could happen in their community that they raised the stone in traumatized memory. The stone itself gives a different story – one less about the victim and more about the killer, who was, it seems, the son of her employer and father of her unborn child. Certainly, the writer was clear on his identity. A prominent Quaker named Elijah Waring, he set the stone to face the suspect's house, out of alignment with the neighbouring headstones. Such biblical fury. Such Nonconformist fire, even here in an Anglican churchyard. It feels like a glimpse of industrial Neath: that 'accursed pandemonium' of coal and copper which, on his visit in 1854, had George Borrow evoking Hieronymus Bosch ('the powerful but insane painter') as he sought to describe its soot-black swamps, its tramways worked by 'savage-looking people', the smoke erupting from 'immense stacks of chimneys surrounded by grimy diabolical-looking buildings' – and all of this, what was worse, on a Sunday.

'They caught him in the end,' says the man behind the counter, in Cadoxton Stores across the road. He is speaking through a surgeon's mask. 'Well, I don't know. I think they did. I'm not from by here, me.'

It is not until you reach Hirfynydd, the hill running northeast away from Neath, that you first encounter Sarn Helen. A grass-striped track framed by broken walls, it follows the ridge through puddles and swamps, over occasional passages of stone once laid down by Roman legionaries. Some of them still have a distinct surface, with neat kerbs to either side. Sarn Helen translates as 'Helen's Causeway' – the Helen in question being Elen Luyddog: princess, saint and subject of 'The Dream of Macsen Wledig', one of the tales written down in the twelfth and thirteenth centuries and later collected in *The Mabinogion*. This tells of the Roman emperor Macsen, 'the fairest man, and the wisest, and the best suited to be emperor of all his predecessors', who, one day, while resting from a hunt near Rome, falls asleep and dreams of crossing mountains, plains and seas to 'the fairest island in the world', where, in a magnificent castle, 'the fairest that anyone had ever seen', he finds a maiden of such dazzling beauty that, on waking, he can think of nothing else. Soon he does little apart from sleep, just to be able to gaze upon her. This being the emperor, a plan is required; and so it is advised by the wisest men of Rome that messengers be sent to the 'three regions of the world' – that is, Africa, Asia and Europe – to discover this enchanting lady.

In the manner of tales, two missions fail, but a third arrives in Britain; its messengers cross Snowdonia and at last reach Caernarfon, where, happily, they find Helen single, sitting in a red-gold chair. Accordingly, Macsen rouses his army, seizes Britain from Beli son of Manogan and marries Helen at the first advantage. Helen is a virgin, a good Caernarfon girl. The following day she claims her maiden fee, which includes 'great roads' to join together forts in Caerleon, Carmarthen and her home town.

So, the tale suggests, was born Sarn Helen.

Which is, of course, a lot of nonsense. Though Macsen, otherwise Magnus Maximus, may have married Elen Luyddog – he was a commander in Segontium (Caernarfon) – he was, in fact, proclaimed Emperor of the Western Empire by the British garrison in AD 383, centuries after the Roman invasion. His subsequent departure for Gaul was an effective withdrawal of forces from the province: the end, not the beginning, of Roman rule.

This track climbing gently among meadow pipits and lately shorn ewes belongs to the early years of the Roman occupation. South Wales, it is true, did not fall lightly – the Silures resisted for thirty years, even defeating the Second Legion – but the Romans built their fort in Neath, probably, in A D 74, so the road must date from around this time. It is straight in stretches, sometimes rutted by bicycles and off-road vehicles. Here big lambs go springing away, arching like dolphins above the brown-flowering rushes. Here saplings seeded from the forestry ahead have escaped the tireless teeth of the sheep, defended by a scrap of wall or by an abandoned bale of wire.

Turning, looking back to the south, it is not hard to imagine this landscape as the Romans might have found it. Above Môr Hafren – the Bristol Channel – the cloud is breaking, spreading into light, revealing a regular, stratospheric whiteness and narrow lengths of pale blue. The sun finds the water of Swansea Bay – Mumbles a protective arm flung against the big Atlantic swell. And, inland from this generous harbour, the Vale of Neath lies rich with silt, its river wandering, navigable, between the richly wooded hills.

Sarn Helen was extractive, let's just say it. It leaves lush and sheltered Neath with the major purpose of discovering wealth and carrying it elsewhere. In which respect, it is of a piece with much of the infrastructure Wales has known. Look, say, at a map of the Great Western Railway in the days before the Beeching cuts and you see venules, arterioles: tiny vessels infesting the Valleys, feeding away by means of the main lines to Fishguard, Liverpool, Swansea, Cardiff and London, the heart itself. The roads and the railways, they say everything about a country's development. The question is: do these form a network, linking the regions and the regions' settlements, or do they resemble a collection of drainage basins, flowing away to the borders and the ports? Perhaps this is among the reasons why 'The Dream of Macsen Wledig' has endured in Welsh mythology. It would be nice to think of this small country that the first road to run its full length was commissioned by an empress-saint to bring together, even to conceive, a nation.

The reality, alas, is the perfect reverse.

The forestry continues for two and more hours – the track mostly straight between the blue-green spruces, drawn in their habitual ranks. To the right there is an old quarry, where the ruts of the bicycles congregate. Two motorbikes come creeping past, their wheels half-lost in a peat-coloured puddle halfway to becoming a canal. The riders wave and carry on. Their noise subsides eventually. Beneath the trees is an acidic desolation: needles, occasionally a tumbled branch. Only the verges give some sense of Hirfynydd as it might be, without conifers, sheep or people; they fight for the light with such determination that often their trees make the track into a tunnel: birches, rowans and moss-fattened oaks, with willows in the damper spots. In their gaps is an abundance of flowers: St John's wort, its yellow-gold stars; yarrow, such an effusion of whiteness as any hawthorn might admire; common spotted orchids, each pink petal patterned like a Rorschach test.

Now the forestry parts for rushes, wavy hair-grass and gangling foxgloves, and I almost step on the tail of a slow worm, which whips away, brown-backed, into the marsh.

It strikes me that, on the OS map, only the straightest parts of the track are described as 'Roman road' – although, for these sections to connect, it can only have turned a corner. It is as if Roman is a synonym for straight, or for this merciless sense of purpose, this impaling of the hinterland.

Only once, along Hirfynydd, do I stop for long enough to set down my rucksack. Next to a path that crosses the track is a pole bearing a small round disc, which reads 'Llwybr Illtud

Sant' and 'St Illtud's Walk'. Besides a symbol a little like a castle, there is no further information – though I check for some yards in either direction.

As it happens, St Illtyd (the spelling varies) has for some years been an obsession of mine – to the extent that my daughter, Alice, has 'Illtyd' for her middle name. Illtyd is one of the major figures of the early years of the Age of Saints: the period following the Roman withdrawal during which Wales was actually conceived. If his *Life* – his hagiography – is to be believed, then Illtyd was a Breton, a cousin of King Arthur and, as a young man, commander of the forces of Glamorgan. One day, the royal household of Glamorgan were hunting in the territory of St Catwg and, growing hungry, demanded that Catwg give them food, threatening violence if he did not comply. Illtyd was absent, hawking, at the time. He returned just as the Lord, in wrath at their effrontery, had the rest of the party swallowed by the ground: an event which, naturally, had its effect on him. Once he had recovered his composure, Illtyd drove away his 'most virtuous wife' Trynihid 'as the poison of a serpent' and left to found an oratory in the Hodnant Valley and to pass long periods immersed to the neck in its river's freezing water. Before long, he rose to the position of abbot, a monastery having grown up around him. On one occasion his estranged wife, after years of chastity and charitable work, had the gall to visit her husband, but the Lord struck her blind and blighted her complexion. And so Illtyd lived to a venerable age, fasting, praying, performing miracles and promoting misogyny and religious intolerance, until at last he returned to Brittany to die.

His *Life*, however, is not to be believed, any more than is 'The Dream of Macsen Wledig' – or, indeed, most other accounts of the early history of Wales. As the historian G. H. Doble notes, 'We have no right to blacken the character of the saints of the fifth century by repeating about them the diseased fancies of twelfth-century romanticists.' The *Life* of St Illtyd, it would appear, was written in about 1140 by a clerk at Llantwit Major, Illtyd's monastery, in part to exalt its founder and so oppose the claims of certain Norman lords, in part to campaign against the Welsh tradition of permitting priests to marry. 'The Dream of Macsen Wledig', meanwhile, by asserting their traditional descent from the emperor, seems to have been shaped in the thirteenth century to support the claims of the princes of Gwynedd to rule over the whole of Wales. This whole High Medieval period (*c.*1000–1250) is thick with such weaponized history, the past turned into propaganda. The most egregious example, surely, is the slander of the kings of Ulster by the writer and cleric Gerald of Wales, which afflicted the province for centuries. In his *Topographia Hibernica*, written in 1187 in support of Henry II and of his own family's interests, Gerald describes a 'savage and abominable' inauguration ceremony in which the would-be king 'without any sense of shame, or regard to civil prudence, professes himself to be also a beast': that is, he has sex with a horse, which then is slaughtered, cut up and boiled. He proceeds to bathe in this broth, and to drink from it 'without using any vessel' but by 'lap[ping] it up with his mouth'.

Finally, late in the afternoon, the nose of Hirfynydd falls away; the forestry fragments into a labyrinth of tracks and the blasted spaces which are all that tell of the former Nant Hir Colliery. The tips and the draglines are decades gone. The opencast workings lie under white grass, spindling saplings and stretches of scrub. Wind turbines slice at the black-bottomed clouds, each of them, in its place on the hillside, issuing a vast, periodical whisper – like the sails of a ship, like the aeroplane thunder which has polluted the air all day. Their blades shift, feather, turn into the breeze. Behind them are the Brecon Beacons, their glaciated angles, their bare, tawny backs: Fan Llia, Fan Gyhirych and, to the north-east, Pen y Fan, whose opposite face we can see, in part, from our kitchen window at home.

The track drops suddenly out of the trees into the high, shallow valley of Banwen, a Valleys town in miniature – Roman Road, its only street, enclosed by terraces with long, narrow gardens. At either end are patches of waste-ground. On this southern slope, among the willows and willowherb, the cow parsley and the deep-cut streams, a stable serves as a meeting place for children who approach, depart, throw sticks, scuff shoes, take turns caressing the one dark mare. The children's faces are bright with summer. Their voices echo and overlap. Were this a story, then one of them would be reticent, lost in dreams of escape from this village which begins in nothing and ends in nothing, but on this close, late-July afternoon all of them seem busy with the present. One of the larger girls, clipping on a helmet, swings herself bareback on to the horse and leads a procession down Roman Road – the other children skipping or riding their scooters, past the Vauxhalls and Seats lining the pavements, past the satellite dishes on the pebble-dash walls.

At one house, surrounded by cement mixers, breeze-blocks, spades and causeways for wheelbarrows, I ask a builder to spare some water. He squints through his thick-lensed glasses, regrets that he has disconnected the taps.

'But I can go one better,' he says, rooting in a van until he finds his bottle. This he pours carefully into my own. 'There we go! Fresh from Banwen Spring!'

Whistling, he returns to his work.

The air contains the lift of skunk.

Though its colliery, its reason for existence, is gone, somebody has put a lot of effort into Banwen. At the southern end of Roman Road is a pair of gaily coloured mosaics: maps which chart the course of Sarn Helen, through forts at Brecon, Llandovery, Llanio, Trawsgoed, Machynlleth, Dolgellau and Trawsfynydd, on at last to Caerhun, the Conwy Estuary and a blue sea featuring a whale and a galley. At the northern end, opposite the Rugby Club where a few men are sitting with distanced pints, is a Celtic cross in an arching wall, flanked by a couple of olive saplings. A plaque remembers Magonus Sucatus Patricius: Patrick, patron saint of Ireland, who was, it says, born right here and not in Cumbria after all. Both of the monuments are recently built. Both, like other regenerative initiatives across the former South Wales coalfield, would seem to be efforts to recast history – to look past Banwen Colliery, once one of the largest anthracite mines in the world, a place of tramways, spoil tips and barely so much as a blade of grass, to a place of saints and Roman legions, a place whose street, far from ending in nothing, led to the sea in both directions: a place which has been imagined and imagined and so, perhaps, can be imagined again.

It may work.

Something has to.

Already, in South Wales, this has been a catastrophic year, doubly defined by the same broader crisis. Of course, there has been Covid-19: a zoonosis linked, says the UK Parliament, to 'increases in animal farming and encroachment into natural habitats due to climate change, land clearance for agriculture and expanding urban developments'. Like so many other afflictions, from depression to heart disease, Covid-19 has ravaged the Valleys, exploiting the health and demographic vulnerabilities born of the end of coal and heavy industry. By May, the five highest infection rates in all Wales and England were to be found in Rhondda Cynon Taf, Merthyr Tydfil, Newport, Cardiff and Swansea, with Blaenau Gwent and the Vale of Glamorgan only slightly further down the list. And then, just a month before the pandemic, as it can be easy to forget, Wales had by far its wettest February on record, with Storms Ciara, Dennis and Jorge concluding by far the warmest winter on record – Europe-wide some 3.4°C above the 1981–2010 average.

These storms brought turmoil across South Wales. Climb on to the head of St Patrick's cross, crane above the nearby trees and you might just see into the Rhondda, where, in Tylorstown, Wattstown, Pontygwaith and Clydach Vale, 'legacy' coal tips collapsed into landslides with nightmare echoes of the 1966 Aberfan Disaster. Soar to the height of that circling kite, that gaunt and V-tailed form against the clouds, and you could surely see Pontypridd, where the Taf filled the high street shops with five feet of filthy water – more than a foot above its previous record – and residents fled their homes by boat and the posses-sions of lifetimes were abandoned on pavements in sodden and hopeless heaps.

That Saturday night I remember well. I had been working late at my partner's café. It must have been almost twelve o'clock when I came to the bridge across the Usk in Brecon, and froze in the face of the river's scale – of its monstrous, light-streaked back, the world that it foretold.

*

'The amount of moisture in the air,' says Marie Ekström, 'is related to atmospheric pressure and temperature. Broadly, you can disregard pressure – it doesn't vary that much, with the full weight of the atmosphere above us – but temperature is a big factor. The warmer the air is, the more moisture can exist as a gas, so the more a water body will evaporate. Of course, if you haven't got a large water body around, that's not going to be the

case, but here we are surrounded by water, so you're going to see a direct response.'

Dr Ekström is Research Fellow in Climate Change Impacts at the School of Earth and Ocean Sciences, Cardiff University: an expert in regional climate science and projections, with a particular focus on extreme rainfall.

We are speaking on Zoom in April 2021.

'That doesn't necessarily mean,' she says, 'that you'll get more rainfall per se, because you still need the mechanism for rainfall to occur. So you can have what's known as orographic rainfall, which everyone in Wales is very familiar with. When you have an air mass that moves up and over mountains, of course, as it's being pushed up, it cools down and that means condensation is occurring and you've got rainfall. So if you've got more water as gas in the air then more rainfall will occur.'

'What about Storm Dennis, then?' I ask. 'In February last year? What sort of mechanisms would have resulted in so much rain falling in such a short period of time?'

'So,' she says, 'that's all to do with how strong that updraught is. And to do with how fast the storm is moving. Storm Dennis was a cyclone, an extratropical cyclone, one of these low-pressure systems that come in from the Atlantic. If a cyclone like that just sits and spins and pulls in these different air masses which keep feeding it, you will get a lot more water in a single location.'

Marie speaks briskly, carefully, her Swedish origins in evidence only at the edges of certain words. Her instinct is technical, or seems to be, and her approach speaks entirely of moderation. When I mention a report on the BBC News in which Professor Liz Bentley, Chief Executive of the Royal Meteorological Society, warned that the South Wales Valleys could see a 50 per cent increase in heavy rainfall over the next ten years, Marie and I spend fully twenty minutes on her shared screen, considering *graphs and seas of figures, while she talks about the issues around 'downscaling' – the process, as one of her papers explains, 'of translating information from global climate model simulations to a finer spatial resolution' – and the range of uncertainty inherent in any such conclusion.*

Within this, however, on two or three occasions she makes reference to RCP8.5: the high-emissions, 'worst-case' climate scenario.

'Are you suggesting,' I ask at one point, 'that RCP8.5 is . . . ?'

'It's quite representative of our behaviour, I would say,' Marie says, without hesitation. She pauses, then gives a quick, bleak laugh. 'I don't see a lot of evidence that we're putting much effort into curbing our emissions. It's certainly not happening so far. We keep increasing them, at an alarming rate . . . I mean, RCP8.5 is a very high-level emissions scenario, but it is the scenario that agrees most closely with observed cumulative CO2 emissions. It does extend quite far into the future, so that's not to say that there won't be a change, but I don't think we've got a lot of time left to act.'

'When you say "act", I say, "act" to avoid what?'

'Well, if we want to get anywhere close to RCP2.6, which I think we have blown already anyway. RCP2.6 is a really low-impact scenario – if we stay under, sort of, 1.5°C warming . . .'

'Correct me if I'm wrong,' I say, 'but last year the global temperature was 1.25°C above the pre-industrial average and, as I understand it, we've already emitted enough greenhouse gases to cause an increase of at least another 0.2°C . . . If that's right, are we not effectively at 1.5°C already?'

'Yeah,' says Marie. 'Yeah . . . if you were to take what has been invested, what we are committed to via emissions. I don't think that anyone in climate science thinks we're going to hit those targets. I don't think we're going to stay under 2°C global warming, with what we're doing. I can't see that we're putting any of the large-scale measures in place by which we can avoid it. It's change on a scale we're just not grasping. It is really frightening . . .'

A change has come over Marie's voice. She remains measured, as ready as ever to summon up technical models and analysis, but there is a weariness now in her tone, a resignation, maybe even an anger.

'So,' I ask, 'if, God forbid, we approach warming of 3°C or something of that order, would you . . . just expect to see an intensification of those trends that we are seeing at the moment?'

'Intensification is a given,' she says. 'Generally, you would expect winters to get wetter and summers probably to get drier, because of the greater evaporative losses during summertime. Storms will increase. The gust wind speeds will increase. So that will have a lot of impact on built infrastructure. Storm surges will become a big problem. Rainfall . . . The intensity will increase, for sure, but will the number of events increase? That is not a given. And connecting rainfall to flooding is not necessarily straightforward because it depends so much on the catchment itself. But it's not meaningful to think about "back to normal" because we're only going in one direction, so it's not going to get better. We're only going to see more flooding.

'Another thing that's very much on the radar for many climate scientists is what's called post-tropical cyclones. That's when a tropical cyclone doesn't die out but starts to enter the mid latitudes: the more temperate areas, outside of the tropics . . . If it undergoes what's known as transition, it starts to pull these different air masses in. So it's not only a tropical cyclone with all the energy that has, it's also starting to pull down the polar air masses, to meet the tropical air masses. Sandy, for example, which struck North America in 2012. That was a post-tropical cyclone. And the indications are that those are starting to become a risk

*on our side of the Atlantic. There was one which touched Ireland
in 2017, but we've never had a full impact from one of those
storms – and they could be really destructive because they're not
just rainfall. They'll probably come with a big storm surge, and
hurricane-force winds that we haven't experienced here before, so
they would be completely different to what the natural environment and the built environment have known.'*

'*And ... they could hit now?' I ask.*

'*They could hit now.'*

'*And what other effects might we expect?'*

'*Well,' says Marie, 'because it's an atmosphere-ocean system,
we need to worry about the ocean as well. Of course, there are
longer-term things like if the Gulf Stream shuts down because
of all the glacial water flushed in – then, all of a sudden, it will
get very cold up here. But among the key concerns is all of those
organisms in the ocean that form calcium carbonate: organisms
with shells. As the oceans get more acidic their shells will dissolve,
leading to a mass extinction. It's all interconnected, and we're far
away from understanding the natural systems sufficiently to know
what unforeseen consequences might happen to food sources.*

'*I don't think the UK's the worst place to be in a climate scenario, because it is very moderated by the ocean. I'm probably
more worried about countries which are borderline sustainable.
Everyone who lives there will have to move somewhere else, and
the conflict that will come from that ... But, even here, the rate of
change is just so vast. Of course, people can always move. We can
change our buildings, our infrastructure. But other species will
find it much, much harder. It all depends how much the climatic
window in which they are comfortable is shifting. Really, we don't
know how vulnerable our systems are. And, anyway, this is just
one of many threats to natural habitats which are being squeezed
more and more.'*

'What's your advice, then?' I ask. 'What do we do?'

'Well,' says Marie. 'There needs to be a systematic response on a government level, which we won't get unless we vote for parties which put that above anything else, and I can't see that happening either in the UK or the US . . . I don't think we appreciate how drastically we need to change. Really, the future looks pretty dire. It scares me – a lot. It seems to me that humans are no better than any animal. We just use, use, use without thinking about the consequences. If any of the runaway effects happen, who knows where we'll end up? If we lose the biodiversity. If we lose our soils . . . The ecosystems are core to everything and if we overuse them, we can't exist.'

*

From the rushes and thistles of Coelbren Fort, half a mile to the north of Roman Road, Sarn Helen steers towards the north-east. According to the map, it ought to exist as a track in the fields around Tonyfildre Farm – although, in fact, there is nothing to be seen except the ruts of a tractor, cutting their way among the sheep and the cattle, the chickens, their chicken-house tucked into a hedge, and the swallows come for their evening's insects, darting a half-inch over the ground. That smell on the stirring air, that warm, heavy must of fleece and dung and masticated grass – it stops me, momently, carries me direct, past the years of the sawmill, to the years at Llanhowell, the farm where we lived when I was a child.

There was always going to be a point of transition, a point where the Valleys changed into the hills; it is surprising only that it should be so distinct. As the footpath doglegs on to a lane, so it passes Cefngwaunhynog: a farm of grey-tin sheds and silo, gathered in the shelter of a gang of Scots pines – ordinary except that, facing the yard, there is a line of terraced houses. Once there

must have been a coal pit here. A couple of the houses are all but
derelict – a dog erupts from the second door to leap, hysterical,
against his chain. Another has had its front wall replaced by a
pair of tall barn doors. But the two houses in the middle have
been knocked together, drained and extended, front and back.
Their double-glazed windows look across the desolate grazing
and dense, wet woods of the Banwen Valley to the wind turbines
on the ridge of Hirfynydd, turning in the pearl-coloured sky.

2

Coed y Rhaiadr to Y Gaer

30 July 2020

Soldiering out of the upper Nedd Valley, a mile or so to the north of Ystradfellte, you see Maen Madoc in silhouette: a finger of sandstone ten feet tall, standing alone in its patch of moor, its golden grass and rushes and heather. The clouds are luminous, cirrocumulus. The planes continue as they did all night – though passenger numbers are said to have fallen by 75 per cent. It is only as you come to the stone that you might discern, on its southern face: 'DERVAC(IVS) FILIVS IVSTI (H)IC IACIT' ('Of Dervacus, son of Justus. He lies here'). You might suppose it a Roman memorial, given the road and the Marching Camp hidden among the nearby spruces – or, if nothing else, proof of cultural continuity into the Age of Saints.

The spruces shiver in the morning breeze.

Far to the south, past the small, stony Nedd and another spruce plantation, Coed y Rhaiadr, mist laps over the slopes of Hirfynydd, enveloping the wind farm – its still-turning blades.

The collapse of the Western Roman Empire quite inverted

Western Britain. For much of the period of Roman rule – AD 43 to 410 – traffic between Britannia and the Continent had con-centrated on the Strait of Dover, where a Roman fleet, the Classis Britannica, provided some protection. Without that fleet, with the gathering danger posed in the east by the Angles, Jutes and Saxons, the Western Seaways began to recover: a network of routes, much disrupted by the Romans, which centred on the Irish Sea but extended north as far as the Orkneys and south, along the Atlantic fringe, to Galicia and beyond. The use of the Seaways dates at least to the Mesolithic period. After 4000 BC, in the Neolithic, they spread megalithic architecture: such passage graves and gallery graves as can be found on all these shores. In the Iron Age, they spread new techniques in textile-making and metalwork, pottery and grinding corn. Now, with the beginning of the Age of Saints, this era of continental chaos, they spread refugees.

The uncial letters carved into Maen Madoc, itself quite possi-bly a megalith, are coated in yellowish and grey-blue lichen; they are large and clumsy, with several among them back to front or upside down. Even so, they reveal a whole age. 'HIC IACIT': 'Here lies'. This formula on memorial stones arose in Italy in the late fourth century and, over the succeeding decades, became widely adopted in Gaul, particularly in the Lyons-Vienne area, the tradi-tional home of Gallic Christianity, and in the Rhineland where, at Trier, Macsen Wledig had his capital. The assumption, then, must be that Dervacus was neither a Roman nor Romano-Briton. More probably, he was a Gallo-Roman Christian, one of the multitudes who, from the early fifth century, fled the Barbarian invasions of Gaul – in this case, sailing north around Cornwall to land somewhere on the West Wales coast, to follow the Roman roads inland, finishing, at last, on this bleak bit of hill.

*

Maen Llia, the second great stone belonging to this part of the Brecon Beacons, appears as a notch in the hard blue sky, like a point of balance for its gaping valley. And to its right, as if for scale, my friend Christopher Meredith is leaning on his hazel sticks. The comparison is not quite fair. Chris is an admirable figure of a man – he has, beneath his raked straw hat, the wiry frame of the inveterate swimmer – but the stone, in shape like an arrowhead, is twelve feet tall and nine feet wide. Given its geometric relationship with three Bronze Age monuments elsewhere in the valley, it must have been marking this route through the mountains for about 4,000 years. In its long, damp shadow I sink to the grass, scratch at the bites of the infernal midges that, for much of the night, had me trapped in my bivvy bag, then ease off my boots and sweat-sodden socks to massage my yellowish, blistering feet.

'I'm told,' I say, though the memory is doubtful, 'that legionaries' sandals only lasted a week.'

'Bloody hell,' says Chris, 'and replace your soldiers every three, was it?'

The thought takes him back to his childhood in Tredegar – in the Sirhowy Valley, due east of Banwen. His father, he says, would use a razor blade to pare the dead skin from his feet: a skill he probably learnt in the Second World War, serving in Burma as a Marine. As a labourer then a foreman at the Ebbw Vale Steelworks, he would often work on top of the coke ovens, his ankles bound to keep the heat out of his trousers, his feet protected only up to a point by the conveyor-belt webbing he would nail to his furnace clogs.

It is, at first, a little unreal to be walking again with Chris in the mountains. For most of this year, with Covid-19, the Beacons have been closed above the fence-line; there were just too many people ignoring the lockdown, wanting to be out in the unprecedented spring – its 626 hours of sunshine quite eclipsing the previous record of 555. Chris, it is true, seems much as ever. A professor emeritus, as well as one of the most respected poets and novelists in Wales, he has earned his self-possession. He talks at once with an academic measure, with Tredegar's open 'o's and extended 'a's, and with the fullness to Welsh words and names of a man who learnt the language in his early twenties and has now been bilingual for decades. The problem, clearly, lies with me. Like some old farmer of the Radnorshire hills too long starved of company, I find myself twitching and dodging his eye; I find that I think before I speak and so lose the imme-diacy, the rhythm in our talk.

But then we arrive in the *bwlch* – the pass – and here we pause, because you must. To the north and east, the mountains continue – grand and sinuous in the high, fierce sunlight, bare as they have been since the Neolithic. But beneath them, within them, is the Senni Valley, life brimming from its long, deep hollow – from its small fields, many of them striped with hay, from its hedges and hedges unravelled into hawthorns, from its tree-shrouded brook and its sprawling farms and its banks of rowan and birch and bracken.

It restores our rapport in a single stroke.

'As a kid,' says Chris, as he leans on his sticks, 'I would go up to Trefil, you know, north of Tredegar. You walk through that moonscape of quarries and moorland. Then suddenly you come to the edge of the hill and you're looking down into Breconshire, and ... it's like this. It's like Eden. The council estate where I grew up, there wasn't a tree there to be seen. Not one. The only hedges were up at the cemetery. So you had this idea of this wonderful place, just there, just over the hill ...'

As the track falls over these contours, you can hardly wonder that so many South Wales industrialists took their titles

and their fortunes and bought estates this side of the mountains – from the Morgans of Morgantown to the Crawshays of
Cyfarthfa, from the Baileys of Nantyglo to the Evans-Bevans
of Neath, owners of Banwen Colliery. Cwm Du, this tribu-
tary of the Senni Valley where the track twists east to meet a
small, arched bridge, would be enough to convince anyone. Its
stream weaves, tumbles over glistening falls, between broad
pebble beaches and banks of red soil topped with clusters of
yellow Welsh poppies. The slopes are high, striated cliffs and
hanging woods, where the sheep cannot climb, of pines and
rowans, whitebeam, ash. From the bridge, which was gutted
by the February storms, Chris and I look into the trees and try
to locate the source of a screaming mew: a buzzard, surely, if a
little too shrill.

It brings to mind the previous Sunday when, on Craig Cerrig
Gleisiad, the great, gouged bowl at the top of this valley, another
friend and I were watching a buzzard circling drowsily near the
bottom of the cliff – too near, clearly, to a peregrine's nest. The
male appeared, climbed at velocity, hovered a moment on his
knife-like wings. He was above us by hundreds of feet, then he
was below us by hundreds of feet. There was no apprehensible
stoop. He might just have materialized, feathers wide, inches
over the buzzard's back.

Mountain ponies watch from the skyline.

Sheep creep patiently over the slopes.

'This one time in the hot mill,' Chris remarks. He worked
in Ebbw Vale himself for a time. 'Did I ever tell you this? Well,
sheep only needed a gap in the fence to get in, and there were
usually some because the blokes were always dodging a few
hours' work . . .' He laughs. 'It must have been an afternoon shift.
One of my jobs as a labourer was to stand by the little steps that
led up to the delivery table in front of the reheating furnace. The

man with the oxygen lance was up there and the job was to stop
anybody else going up. I mean, it was meaningless. There was
nobody about. We weren't rolling metal or anything. So I was
just standing there, being a policeman, and one of these sheep
came wandering along. It looked a bit like how you'd imagine a
partisan in the old Yugoslavia in 1943: bits of wool hanging off
it, you know, looking very ragged and mean. It was just one of
those moments. The whole place was completely deserted, and
all you get when it's quiet like that is this hiss of steam from the
various pipes – and then this bloody sheep comes wandering up
like, like something out of *High Noon* . . .'

We continue north among small, scruffy hawthorns.

'The big change in Tredegar, then,' I ask, 'would that have
come with the closure of the steelworks?'

Chris inhales through naked teeth. 'Well . . .' he says. 'Yes . . .
I don't know. I'm very suspicious of accounts of history that
talk about turning points. When you look closer there's almost
always a bigger, slower process at work. Like, if you look at the
figures, the decline of the South Wales coal industry starts
in 1913. But even so, there was a point when these places like
Tredegar, which had been very thinly populated, just forestry
and smallholdings, when they got turned over, literally – like a
garden, dug up and turned over. And '79, when the Tories came
to power . . . Before that, you know, Labour had been trying
to run down the steel industry in Ebbw Vale for a while, but
they were trying to do it at a human pace, a pace that wouldn't
cause too much damage. The Thatcher government, they didn't
care. It didn't matter to them. What happened was, a process
that was already under way was accelerated and distorted cata-
strophically. Suddenly, across a large community, you're rid of
the main means of people earning their living. Your young men
and women haven't got an economy, and you've got this absurd

situation in which they're being told, you know: "You're lazy, get on your bike and go and find a job."

'Well, I had crossed the mountains by that time – I was teaching in Brecon, you know – but my parents were still living in Tredegar and I was still going back there pretty much every week in the late 1970s and early 1980s. When you're at a small distance, you're almost better able to see the change because you see a series of pictures. You're more aware of the difference between them.

'I think, in those hilltop estates, it helped suck a drugs economy into existence. If you get an onslaught like deregulation of the buses, so that people who live in these places, and don't have cars, can't get in and out of the estate after dark . . . if you sell off the council houses and neglect the funding for council accommodation . . . The estate where I grew up, a lot of the houses have just been pulled down because they became of such low value that only housing associations would buy them and they weren't maintained. All of these things coming together, they created really terrible conditions. I mean, we're not talking about people starving, we're not talking about war, but these are damaging, attritional conditions. If you create a situation in which the drugs economy is an easier way for young people to survive, in which that's seen by some as a reasonable way to behave . . . well, I don't think most of those areas have ever really recovered.'

The Western Seaways brought refugees, and the refugees brought Christianity. Not that Christianity was new to Wales – of the three third-century martyrs named by Gildas in *De Excidio et Conquestu Britanniae*, two, Julius and Aaron, seem to have been executed in Caerleon – but, in this overwhelmingly rural area, it is unlikely ever to have been widespread, nor long to have survived the Roman withdrawal. Christianity, under the Roman Empire, was very much an urban religion, while paganism belonged in the countryside, the *pagus* (also, incidentally, the root word for Powys, which has never altogether got to grips with towns). There is evidence for some continued practice, chiefly in Caerwent, the only *civitas* capital of any significance in Wales, where a small church was built in the early sixth century; but in so far as the religion survived there at all it must have been revitalized by other Romano-Britons fleeing the Barbarian raids on towns like Silchester and Cirencester. As with the Western Seaways themselves, the general trend was one of reversion. In the Iron Age, before the Roman Conquest, the peoples of Wales had principally inhabited the uplands in, or in the region of, a hill fort, at 400–1,000 feet above sea level. Now, in the Age of Saints, this Celtic life more or less resumed. There were multiple tiny kingdoms led by the likes of Gwrtheyrn and Maelgwn Gwynedd, who, if they did not entirely reverse the Romans' fondness for dwelling in valleys, kept their fortified farmsteads to the fringes of the hills as they sought to withstand the political collapse and the chaos wrought by the Anglo-Saxon, Irish and Pictish invasions.

This, then, was the situation met by the Gauls who, in the early years of the Age of Saints, arrived on the Western British shores: refugees, but not simply refugees, and some, quite possibly, not refugees at all. There was, at this time, a monastic movement pervading Gallic Christianity inspired by the 'Desert Fathers' – principally St Anthony of Egypt who, in the late third century, spent twenty years alone in a remote, abandoned fort. This movement was ascetic, mystical, *Eastern* – unlike anything the West had known. In fourth-century Gaul the central figure was St Martin of Tours, who seems to have known Macsen Wledig during his years in Trier and to have had a particular connection with his empress. In his *Dialogues* concerning St Martin, Sulpicius Severus describes how 'she matched the woman in the Gospels by watering the feet of the holy man with her tears and wiping them with her hair'. Whether this empress was Elen Luyddog, Severus does not make clear – although another story proposes that, after Macsen's death, Elen and her sons travelled back to Caernarfon, there to seed monasticism. If this is true, then she was not alone – in general terms, at least. As the early memorial stones make clear, numerous Christians made a similar journey. And, as a result, fifth- and sixth-century Wales did not see only a reversion to Iron Age customs. It also saw the dawn of Celtic Christianity: a fusion, in the area now covered by Breconshire, Monmouthshire and Herefordshire, of Gallic, Romano-British and some Irish influences. It saw the great monastic houses of Llancarfan and Llantwit Major – the latter founded by St Illtyd, who may himself have spent time in monastic communities near Marseilles. It saw the 'saints': multitudes of holy men and women who, like their Gallic inspirations, set out alone from the places they knew, at once to escape the evil, anxious world and to seek a cave or a mountaintop, a wind-scourged island or an overgrown valley – in a word, the wilderness.

Perhaps Dervacus, son of Justus, had reached his destination after all.

It is early in the afternoon when Chris and I pass Forest Lodge. We leave the shade of its overgrown hedges and emerge on Mynydd Illtyd, 'Illtyd's Mountain', or rather hill, or upland expanse of bracken and gorse, birch-twined bog and eruptions of bedrock. This being the common above our house, I must have spent months of my life up here, walking in enormous loops, building scenes and, out of them, stories. It was here that I began to attend to Sarn Helen. It was here that I developed my passion for Illtyd – for trying to understand who he actually was.

The *Life* of St Samson of Dol, composed in the early seventh century, is by far the most contemporary (and, presumably, reliable) of the hagiographies. Here, Illtyd is described as 'of all the Britons the most accomplished in all the Scriptures, namely of the Old and New Testaments, and in those of philosophy of every kind, of geometry namely, and of rhetoric, grammar and arithmetic, and of all the theories of philosophy. And by birth he was a most wise magician, having knowledge of the future.' Which has led to suggestions that he was a druid – or at least, which would hardly be surprising, that the pagan priesthood played some part in the religious fusion of this time. (To judge by the number of scribes to have changed the word *magicus* to *magnificus* in the manuscript, this is a thought that has often caused discomfort.) For all that I have tried in the past few years, Illtyd is not an easy man to pin down. Like King Arthur, his putative cousin, he surfaces in tale after tale. In this one, he is driving back the sea with his staff. In that one, along with Catwg and Peredur, he is one of the custodians of the Holy Grail, cognate with Sir Galahad. In the end, perhaps, it can only be said with confidence that Illtyd died in approximately 525 and that he was abbot of the monastery at Llantwit Major, arguably the first great seat of learning in Britain. But then, since it hinges on no supernatural incident, there may be something to be said as well for the Breconshire conclusion to his story: this is that, having taught for many years, he packed his cup and his books of prayer and himself walked until he found this hill, his own 'place of resurrection'.

Here, in an island of seventeen fields cut from the middle of the common land, is an almost-ring of haggard pines following an embankment two feet deep. Inside are some crumpled graves, a few old headstones of which several have fallen and, beside them, a low rectangular wall, which is all that remains of Llanilltud Church, demolished in 1995. Here is the thing about the Age of Saints. As remote, as unknowable as the saints themselves might be, their places remain, a continuous present. There is always this point of connection – and the more so in these upland parts of Wales, which were not, as Chris Meredith put it, dug up and turned over. It was in this spot, so the story goes, that the saint chose to spend his final years. He was buried nearby, at Bedd Gŵyl Illtyd – the 'Grave of Illtyd's Feast Day' – where, on the eve of 6 November, locals are said once to have kept a vigil.

It is a story, admittedly, with its problems. Bedd Gŵyl Illtyd, with its two recumbent stones, is demonstrably a Bronze Age burial cairn. In fact, Llanilltud itself is almost certainly a pagan site repurposed by the new religion, having a prehistoric standing stone to the south-west and south-east of the churchyard. And this is not its only curiosity. By and large, the saints had little appetite for missionary work. Their average site is some 300 feet below the average homestead of its time: on the floors of the forested valleys, not on the tops of the hills themselves. And then, of course, it is within spitting distance of a major Roman road. None of which affects the fact that, plainly, this is an early site, but if Illtyd did live here 1,500 years ago, you do have to question his commitment to reclusion.

These days, if Llanilltud receives any visitors it is because it is about 400 yards away from the Brecon Beacons National Park Visitor Centre and Tearooms. With its thronging car park, chrome urinals, picnic tables and souvenirs, the Visitor Centre is not a place of mystery. It is here because the views are spectacular – and it must be said that, with their fifty-foot advantage, the views from Llanilltud are more spectacular again. Llanilltud is encompassed by mountains – from the ice-carved head of Fan Brycheiniog, through Fan Gyhirych, Fan Nedd and Craig Cerrig Gleisiad, whose sides Chris and I were crossing two hours back. It faces Pen y Fan, the crown of them all: the tallest peak in Southern Britain – its sheer north face as if cross-hatched, as if made explicitly three-dimensional by its almost-horizontal strata and the vertical splay of its gullies and landslips. And, as if these mountains weren't enough, these miles of moor and teeth of rock and reaching woods and projected clouds, from the ridge of Cefn Cyff appears a whole new range: the long and barren crest of the Black Mountains, following the course of the River Wye, of the ground as it falls and spreads into England.

Llan: a word which once meant enclosure (as in *gwinllan*, vineyard) but which, in the Early Middle Ages, came to mean specifically an enclosed burial ground and so, by extension, a church. Visit almost any of these early *llannau* and you can hardly miss their position in the landscape. When you climb the steps into the churchyard at Llanelieu, the church and the scarp of Rhos Dirion both rear suddenly above you; the experience can be overwhelming. I have yet to sit in Rhulen Church, deep in its cleft between the Radnorshire hills, and not feel a sense of absolute calm. Some of these places are harder to grasp, and for me, for a time, Llanilltud was one. These days, though, I come here often. Even during lockdown, with the churches closed, I would cycle on the lane to this patch of private ground, to stand before the absent altar – which is, I suppose, a mysterious habit for someone who could never have called himself a Christian. I can only say that, more often than not, to be alone at a *llan* like this will bring me a sense of peace, of lucidity – and that this must have been the case for the saints as well. I can only suggest that the early Christians, and in this case the earlier pagans, chose these places for an innate awe, tranquillity or other form of sacred power. Perhaps it was thoughts of asceticism that made me miss the obvious fact that Llanilltud is all about elation. Sometimes it will bring me such a sense of uplift that I find I have forgotten to breathe. Sometimes my mind will clear for minutes at a time, seeming to leave nothing but a blazing light. Certainly, whoever its founder, he chose this site because here he experienced God.

'As a kid,' Chris says again, once we have roamed through Darwin, Dostoevsky, local gossip and the misdeeds of publishers, 'there was a walk I used to do. I'd go up past – it was a hilltop estate, you know – past a pond and up on to an area called Twyn yr Hyddod, and walk south along the edge of the valley, high up, opposite Troedrhiwgwair, where my mother was brought up.'

We are neither of us speaking so brightly now. The lane stretches, shimmering, ahead of us. It seems to contort in the feverish heat. The brim of my hat is beginning to sag. The sweat in my eyebrows keeps touching my glasses, then running down one or other lens. This is, in fact, as time will prove, the second-hottest day of 2020 – and 2020, jointly with 2016, although without the warming effect of El Niño, will prove the hottest year globally since records began.

'By that time,' says Chris, 'the coal industry was largely done. It was like the wreckage on a beach, you know, after the tide's gone out – though, now I think of it, there was still one opencast mine. We called it the Dinosaur because it left this long, scaly back of dirt and shale right along the ridge of the mountain. We used to go and play on the heavy machinery. Anyway, this place to the south, that was never working in my lifetime. It was where they used to crank the waste from Bedwellty Pits – on a wire, you know, what my father used to call an aerial flyway.

I mean, there was no pit waste left. It was all grass, and a few scrubby trees, and bits of cliff I used to climb. My memory may be exaggerating – this was forty ... fifty years ago – but there were these two enormous drums, which the cables would have gone round. The sides were pieces of cast iron – nine feet across maybe, something like that – and the timbers that connected them were like railway sleepers, these enormous pieces of wood. Well, the one drum was wrecked – the timber was all but rotted away – but the other one was pretty intact, and there were these triangular gaps in the iron that were quite easily big enough to get through ...

'I didn't know what the thing was for. It could have been an ancient monument, or a tumulus, or an early-medieval church, it didn't matter. Except it mattered in the sense that it had that feel. I'd get in there and sit and ... it was the same experience. It was the same as going into a church.'

There are people walking and picnicking here, in the spaces in the bracken; their vehicles and litter are scattered down the verges. A man from Port Talbot expresses surprise when we explain that he is standing on a Roman road; he relays the information to his dachshund. Some children are laughing at the prim alpacas belonging to Blaenrheon Farm. A couple of families are throwing a frisbee – awkwardly, as it seems to me, as if unsure if they should be socially distanced, if the spring's constraints were really enough to bring the pandemic under control.

Where the course of Sarn Helen disappears from the map, Chris and I bear north with the fence-line, heading for the slope of Twyn y Gaer: one of the numerous local hills crowned with the earthworks of an Iron Age fort.

'That feeling,' says Chris, 'I don't think it's connected with Christianity, or even religion. I mean, you might call it a religious feeling, although I don't think that means a lot unless you link it up with a system of belief. It's just a powerful moment of stillness, or ... perhaps stillness is never possible. Perhaps it's an illusion. Everything's in flux. But an ability to achieve a *sense* of stillness, like those moments in the drum, I do think that you need those, just to apprehend being alive.'

In the earlier stages of lockdown, having a seven- and ten-year-old to teach, my partner Charlie and I decided that forts might make for an interesting subject. We started with the Iron Age. Twyn y Gaer being out of bounds, we forded the Usk in Llanspyddid and made our way up the forestry tracks, through the oaks and newly planted cherries to the highest parts of Coed Fenni Fach. There we launched a series of fruitless expeditions between the rows of conifers, searching for any trace of the site. We were on the point of giving up when we stumbled over a ditch and a bank, into a sudden oval space: a hilltop, flat and panoramic, clear except for a few old stumps. For twenty minutes or half an hour, we tried to imagine the palisade and where its gateway might have been; and the round, thatched houses leaching smoke, with inside maybe a forge or loom; and the boar-like pigs and the goat-like sheep; and the Silures, the people themselves, whom Tacitus describes as dark-skinned and curly-haired, having originally come from the Iberian Peninsula.

Two weeks or so later we set out again – using our daily permissible walk to visit Y Gaer, the Roman auxiliary fort almost at the foot of that same hill. We followed this path along the pebble-lined Ysgir. We tramped through these lowland fields, whose sheep lie in heat-stunned heaps beneath the trees. Here, we noted, was the Cardiff road. Here was a *mansio*: a large stone residence with bath-suite and latrines for accommodating high-ranking officials. Here was a collection of timber buildings: workshops for craftsmen, blacksmiths and tanners, which, so a coin depicting Trajan suggests, were established in the late first and early second centuries. And should some Silurian have somehow missed the point, the verges, like the approaches to the other three gatehouses, would of course have been lined with corpses – mutilated or reduced to their bones.

Now Chris and I stop at the gate to Gaer Farm, where a sign forbids entrance because of the pandemic. Nobody appears to be about. There is no car outside the house: an imposing, starkly modernized place with lawns and patio facing Pen y Fan. Nothing moves in the dusty yard, nor in the sheds and the old stone barns. The walls of the fort still stretch to either side, in some parts ten feet in height, topped with grass and rowans and hawthorns. Through a gap, we can just see a sheep strolling along the *via principalis*, past the site of the great hall used in the winters to exercise the horses of the Ala Hispanorum Vettonum, the resident 500-strong cavalry unit from the Tagus Valley in western Spain.

Two thoughts return from those lessons in lockdown, gathered around the kitchen table with colouring pencils and cardboard for models. The first is that the history of the Usk Valley seems to have been largely a matter for Spaniards. The second, perhaps, is more substantial. A hill fort is secure but a hill fort is anxious; it is watchful, circumscribed, spartan by nature. These forts occur by the hundred in Wales, almost on every suitable hill. They speak of lives in constant peril. And meanwhile, such was their military dominance, the Romans simply built in the valley: here, on this low spur of ground, between this stream and this slender river.

It is a whole new definition of control.

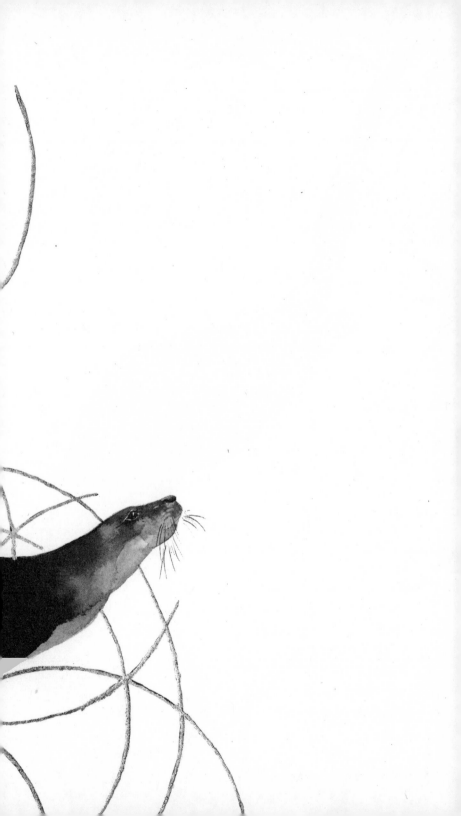

3

Y Gaer to Llandovery

8 September 2020

It is a morning of droplets clinging to your glasses, of the faint pop of water on near-autumnal leaves: the hazels and hawthorns surrounding the lane leading west out of Aberyscir. Mist drags across the slopes of the broad Usk Valley. It hangs from the conifers of Coed Fenni Fach, encloses in silver its Iron Age fort – hides everything, in fact, above Pen-y-Wern Wood, as if this were the background of one of those pictures, those reconstructions by Alan Sorrell with Harlech or Rhuddlan Castle at its heart. For minutes, crossing the heedless Ysgir, passing the motte at Aberyscir Court, this might almost be the Wales that I dreamt as a child, fuelled by a Cymrophile primary school teacher. Then, everything seemed to wait beneath the surface: Arthur, waiting in Craig yr Aderyn; the dragon under Radnor Forest, held in a ring of ancient churches, which would wake should one of those churches be abandoned and visit centuries of fiery vengeance on Cascob, Bleddfa, Dolau, New Radnor.

Here is a chapel turned residential property: a thing of unrelated pieces, of Gothic gate and roller garage and porch befitting a county hall.

Here, on the dull-shining lane near Aberbrân, are an older couple I know from Charlie's café and, once, from a meeting of Extinction Rebellion (XR). The man, lordly in an old fawn coat, begins at once on pollutants in the Usk. The woman, very much thinner and quieter, her rosy face peering from the hood of a cagoule, waits for a space in her husband's talk to ask about the past week's XR actions.

It is hard to know how to answer such questions. There is always the fear of seeming to lecture, or to criticize, or to be some kind of fanatic – and, in a small community, the risk that such impressions might become attached to your children too. Today I opt for a middle course between evasion and full disclosure. Our group, I say, were supposed to go to Cardiff, but we have all of us sat in a Cardiff street and received little more than quizzical interest, even from the South Wales Police. For three days the previous summer we closed Castle Street with a boat and ourselves, and, although we were purposely breaking the law since little else peaceful brings such attention, the only arrest was a teenager who cycled into one of our banners, fell off and turned out to have stolen the bike. At night you would hear police at the Revolution Bar, asking the drinkers to keep it down since people were trying to sleep in the road. And so, this time, we took ourselves to London, to sit together in Parliament Square while speakers exhorted from a makeshift stage between the statues of Peel and Disraeli, while a helicopter clattered overhead and an elderly Scot in a sandwich board bellowed, 'Repent! King Jesus is coming!'

This answer, it seems, is satisfactory.

What I didn't say would be harder to express, more troubled, less anecdotal. I didn't say how few we were: thousands but not tens of thousands. I didn't describe the way it felt, to sit with my friends Jay Griffiths and Henry Shawdon once a Section 14 had been declared – an order under the 1986 Public Order Act, allowing the clearance of public assemblies – and watch the approach of those fluorescent yellow jackets among the placards and the flags with their hourglass stencils. Publicly, deliberately to disobey the law: it is contrary to your every instinct. It is like a rebellion against yourself. I said nothing of the cell in Charing Cross – my second cell in Charing Cross, in fact, the first having been the previous October – its lilac walls with their woodchip dash, the shuttered window set into its door and, opposite, the opaque glass bricks arranged into seven rows of five. I didn't say that, had I not spent two and a half days eating grey baked beans and drinking cups of bitter tea, pacing the minute floor and leaning on the short, angled wall beside the toilet, first with one arm and then with the other, all while absorbing *Madame Bovary*'s despair, then I might not have had this yearning for movement. I might not have troubled to return to Sarn Helen – or at least to these Usk Valley lanes, the course of the Roman road here being lost – and so might not have been in Aberbrân at all.

The Western Seaways brought Christian refugees, and the Western Seaways brought Irish pagans: the likes of the Scotti, whom Gildas describes as emerging from their curraghs 'like dark swarms of worms that emerge from the dark crevices of their holes'. Already, in the fourth century, during the Roman occupation, the Déisi of the south-east coast of Ireland had been plundering – and settling – the west coast of Britain. Dyfed and the Llŷn Peninsula, which lacked Roman infrastructure, were particularly vulnerable. Little wonder, then, that with the Romans gone the attacks intensified. By 410, the end of Imperial Britain, Dyfed was established as an Irish kingdom. Throughout the fifth century, in fact, the Irish were a threat equal to the Barbarians – creating still more refugees as people from South Wales, Devon and Cornwall poured south into Brittany.

A map showing stones inscribed in Ogham, the old Irish alphabet, gives some sense of this Irish world. Naturally, most of these stones are in Ireland itself, with most of those spread along the southern coast, but they can be found as far afield as Scotland and the Isle of Man, Cornwall and even Silchester, in central England, where an Ogham stone was unearthed in 1893 at the bottom of a disused well. After Ireland, though, the largest number are clustered in South-west Wales, with a distinct limb stretching out to the east – following the Roman road, charting an advance into a vacuum of power and, it would seem, into a weak space: a borderland between the Silures and their neighbours, the Ordovices.

A mile or so past Aberbrân, quiet in a gathering drizzle, Trallong comprises a few terraced cottages and one low-energy passivhaus, squeezed beneath the mist of the north side of the valley, along with a phone-box, some ornamental trees and a small, unshowy church. This was rebuilt in 1856, though the churchyard is raised at its edges and curvilinear enough to suggest an early origin. Under the dribbling roof of the porch, the door of the church is locked, of course, but I have been here often enough. Clasped to the wall at the back of the nave is a sandstone slab nearly six feet tall, discovered, when the old church was demolished, serving as a window jamb. Its two fifth- or early-sixth-century inscriptions are neat and plainly legible: one in Latin reading 'CVNOGENNI FILIVS CVNOGENI HIC IACIT' ('Of Cunocennius, son of Cunogenus. He lies here') and one in Ogham, in the right-hand corner, reading 'CVNACENNIVI ILVVETO' – 'ILVVETO', so R. A. S. Macalister explains in *Corpus Inscriptionum Insularum Celticarum*, indicating that this man came from 'a place called Elmet, Elfed, or Elvet'. Above both is a Latin ring cross, incised between the seventh and ninth centuries, which may be an example of 'depaganization'. It is such a fascinating, complex object: an indication, with its Irish name and Latin, Gallo-Roman formula, of a growing association between these very different settlers.

And the Ogham stones of Wales are only part of the evidence. In Llangors Lake, to the east of Brecon, there is an Irish artificial island, a crannog: the only example to be found in the country. You can hire a boat and paddle around it, though landing is prohibited. This conflict, this programme of Irish colonization litters the ancient stories of Wales. In Rhygyfarch's *Life* of St David, the saint's major adversary is the pagan Irish chieftain Bwya. In *De Situ Brecheniauc*, a manuscript written in about 1200, even the Usk Valley road gets a mention. Drawing on much older traditions, it tells of Marchell, daughter of Tewdrig, one of the first Irishmen to settle this area, and her flight from a period of extreme cold. Her journey, in the company of twelve female attendants and 300 men, most of whom freeze to death, takes her along the Usk and Tywi Valleys and so to Porth Mawr, the harbour for St David's. When at last she arrives in Ireland she marries Anlach, a local prince, and subsequently gives birth to Brychan.

Who gave his name to the Kingdom of Brycheiniog.

Which, in turn, gave its name to Brecon.

Last summer in Liverpool, in a Holiday Inn Express otherwise full of Jehovah's Witnesses, Charlie, the children and I

found ourselves watching on television the comedians Paul
Whitehouse and Bob Mortimer fishing in a river of an otherworldly beauty. The Usk, we realized after a moment – a moment
in which we saw it again. Otherworldly is the word. You can see
why Visit Wales might claim that the Usk Valley inspired the
Shire, that idyllic region in *The Lord of the Rings* – and Tolkien, it
seems, did stay in Buckland, and Crickhowell and Crickhollow
are no distant relations. The Usk Valley may be no richer, in its
deep, red soil, its slumbrous cattle, its fields haunted by former
meanders, than the Herefordshire plain fifteen miles to the east;
but the Herefordshire plain is just that, flat. It has abundance
but it lacks definition. It does not wander among folded hillsides,
among the great, swelling bodies of green and gold which are
the Black Mountains and the Brecon Beacons.

It is wealth in all senses, as the houses reflect. In Radnorshire,
to the north and east, there are few examples of architectural
grandeur. There is Doldowlod Hall, to the south of Rhayader:
the mongrel child of a Jacobean mansion and a Victorian
railway station, home to the heirs of James Watt, the Scottish
engineer. There is Cabalva on the southern fringe, home to the
descendants of Sir Josiah John Guest, ironmaster of Dowlais,
Merthyr Tydfil. But, by Usk Valley standards, these are spartan
offerings. A matter of yards to the west of Trallong, a lane runs
long and straight down the hill towards two separate, enormous
houses, built by branches of the same family. One, Penpont, is
all Georgian splendour, hedges trimmed into families of ele-
phants and a maze in the pattern of a Green Man's face. The
other, Abercamlais, is a stiffer affair, more like the setting of
a costume drama. Its three-arched bridge is close enough to
the ford described by Col. W. Ll. Morgan, in his piece on Sarn
Helen in the 1907 *Archaeologia Cambrensis*. It is also, as it turns
out, private – though the builders restoring its parapets do not

seem to mind if I cross, and the lady with the long blonde hair, watching from one of the vast sash windows, seems to give the slightest inclination of her head.

And the terraces of Banwen are just fourteen miles away.

But Banwen belongs to a different world. By history, by geography, the coastal plain of South-east Wales – along with the mines of its hinterland – is a western peninsula of Lowland Britain. Its attention has often been on life beyond the Bristol Channel, not on the mountains at its back. You can see this in the evidence from the Iron Age – particularly in the forts of multiple ramparts common to Devon, Dorset and Somerset, and to Gower, Glamorgan and Gwent. In fact, had the Kingdom of Gwent not defeated Wessex in AD 630 then South-east Wales might well have gone to England. The Usk Valley, arguably, is part of South-west Wales: a cultural area reflected by, if not defined by, the incursions of the Irish. Consider the distribution of church dedications, and multiple examples reveal the same pattern as that of the Ogham stones: a clustering in Pembrokeshire, stretching to the east along the former Roman road. This is true of dedications to the children of Elen Luyddog – the likes of Constantine, whose easternmost dedication is at Welsh Bicknor (Llangystennin) near Ross-on-Wye in Herefordshire – and of dedications to the children of Brychan, many of whom seem to have followed the road west, then sailed to evangelize Devon and Cornwall. Most plainly, it is true of dedications to David – this being a space which, by the Middle Ages, had become formalized as the Diocese of St David's.

As someone from the border parts of Wales, it is easy to get trapped in a story of division. In Wales, after all, there is the standard history, the basic key to national identity: everything was fine, then the English came. It is a narrative of enormous power, and I am as susceptible as anybody else. (My ticket to the 2013 rugby game in which Wales crushed England 30–3 is glued to the wall above my desk.) It is a narrative which contains all of the anguish at the root of this country: the original terror of annihilation. And yet, of course, it is not true – at least, in its implication that Wales has experienced two static conditions, prelapsarian and postlapsarian.

This, for me, is the great joy of the Usk Valley. Here, the standard history shatters. This stone, this fort, this dedication: everything is a jumble of influences – from Gauls to Romans, Irish to Spaniards.

Continue west to the City of St David's and initially you might find yourself baffled. Not only is the city the size of a village, it is lost near the tip of a wind-stripped headland, while its cathedral, its centrepiece, is all but concealed in the narrow Alun Valley. It can be a test for the imagination to orientate everything back to the west, to grasp how, 1,500 years ago when Irish pirates plagued the coast, this would have been an ideal location: a hub of Celtic Christian culture, bound by the sea to the world beyond.

On Trephilip Bridge, above the River Senni, an angler is leaning, considering the water or perhaps the reflections of the alders and sycamores. He is a man in his sixties in a pair of waders, a bucket hat and a camouflage jacket – his rod, assembled, leaning at his side. He scarcely moves as I hobble towards him.

'How are you doing?' I ask, in greeting.

'I am disgruntled,' he says, looking round. His voice, in the local way, makes free use of the 'r'. 'I just went and lost my tackle.'

'I just got bitten by a dog,' I say, and show him the still-oozing holes in my leg.

'Maescar Farm.' He gives a sympathetic nod. 'Bloody terror them dogs are.'

The angler looks back into the trough of the river. The drizzle has stopped now; the surface is clear. A few little trout dart over the stones, cousins to the brace that hang from his hand. Behind us, though it must be three fields distant, though the A4067 runs nearby, you can hear the children of Sennybridge Primary School: a steady shrill of wild excitement, of a second day of autumn term after six months kept at home.

In Llanfaes, probably, my own children are making a similar noise.

It is a sorrow to him, the angler says, that so few of the children come to the rivers. When he was a boy, the Chapel Pool – on the Usk, in Sennybridge – was the swimming place for the entire community, the place where he and his friends would pass their summer holidays. You'll still find otter there, he says. Wait among the trees just behind the Red Lion, where the view takes in both sides of the bend, and you're sure to see the adults landing their fish and, just at the moment, the cubs at play, rolling around together. There is space for them all, so far as he's concerned: the anglers and otters and kingfishers. He feels no sense of competition. If a head pops out of his pool, sleek and dark in its necklace of rings, he will simply take his rod elsewhere. The problem, he says, is the phosphate concentrations – the runoff from free-range poultry units and the granular fertilizer spread on the fields – those and the recent hot, dry springs, which have kept the rivers warm, slow, shallow, ripe to be stifled by sickly green algae. The problem, he says, is the lure of screens and the fact that, with so many more cars on the roads, unsupervised play is so much more dangerous.

Among the leaves of the trees on the banks, above the sharply rising fields, we can just see the tower of Defynnog Church – its grubby white walls, its weathercock. It appears to emerge from a black-green nest: the head of a yew, which is often claimed as the oldest tree in the UK.

The pitch that climbs out of the village of Trecastle might just be the day's first proper Roman road. It begins with the tireless A40 traffic, a bus stop whose buses have long been discontinued and the former school, now an antiques centre – the playground a tangle of horse ploughs, chimney pots and 1970s furniture. A lorryload of hay bales comes creeping down the bank. To either side are culs-de-sac of double glazing and potted geraniums, rotary washing lines and fuel oil tanks. Above one door is a model of a dragon. Against one pavement sits a Subaru Impreza: a car which once, with its alloys and spoiler, was the definition of local cool, but which is mostly now driven by men pushing forty with beanie hats and little beards and bumper stickers still mourning Paul Walker.

Swallows flicker across the roofs.

Hedges begin where the houses end: blackthorn, rose-hips, black-fringed nettles, the fluffy wreckage of rosebay willowherb – those and betony and herb robert, which seem in September to have been flowering forever. The blackberries are sweet and soft. The lane climbs with the ridge through the fields worth mowing into fields awash with rushes, past a division of conifers – all of it vague as the drizzle resumes, as the lane arrives in the lid of cloud where the only indications of the outside world are the shapes of shorn sheep peering through the fences, the red-and-white poles that designate a pipeline and, as ever, the grumbling of aircraft.

Then, suddenly, a wind feels its way from the south and the cloud begins to lift, to fragment. As the lane crosses a cattle grid and becomes the track along Mynydd Bach Trecastell, lowland fields show bright, almost emerald, their valleys banded with luminous mist. A mountain, it must be Fan Brycheiniog, appears in a scrap of azure sky – its back spilling cloud like a waterfall.

Y Pigwn, a pair of Roman marching camps whose earthworks overlay one another so as almost to resemble an eight-pointed star, occupies the summit of this long, barren hill. Such camps were often built in the 70s AD during the Frontinus campaigns, when as many as 30,000 Roman soldiers were brought to bear on the Welsh tribes. Sometimes they were occupied for only one night – though this larger camp is a mile in circumference and even the smaller has space enough to accommodate the tents of an entire legion: *papiliones*, as the tents were known, their flaps recalling butterflies. The place, as part of the initial invasion, would have been chosen for its outlook, which would, very likely, not have been so different nearly 2,000 years ago. Then too the Roman road would have passed east and west. Then too Mynydd Bach Trecastell would have been largely a desolation; these uplands, whose oak and birch were easier to fell than the denser, swampier trees of the valleys, had mostly been cleared for millennia. Then too Fan Brycheiniog would have reared from these hills, a great, sheer wedge of Old Red Sandstone with, to either side, the glacial lakes of Llyn y Fan Fawr and Llyn y Fan Fach. Even the famous legend of Llyn y Fan Fach may have existed in some form. According to the historian John Davies, this tale of a girl who emerges from its water, marries a young man and remains with him happily until three times he strikes her with iron, may remember the threat posed by Iron Age Celts to Wales's earlier inhabitants.

It seems rarely to be understood that these hills and mountains – icons of postcards and Visit Wales posters – are not, in fact, a natural landscape. Live here and they are the shapes of your life, the contours by which you are defined. There is permanence in their skeletal grace. Perhaps I would never have questioned them myself, had it not been, in 2001, for the disaster of Foot and Mouth Disease. That year, at night on Mynydd Epynt, you could see the red eyes of the animal pyres. For months the hilltops were out of bounds, left without livestock, left without people – or only those who kept to the lanes. Sometimes I would drive across Hay Bluff, the Begwns or Llanbedr Hill and stare, in growing fascination, at the fuzz that was rising from the ground: the saplings in uncountable numbers, each one flying a leaf or two, declaring itself hawthorn, birch or rowan.

It was as if they had been waiting 5,000 years for just this opportunity.

It is easy to think of industrial Wales – of 'Little Hell', the slum in Merthyr Tydfil, or the smogs of Swansea's copper works, the river running black through the Afan Valley or the lunar wastes of Dinorwig Slate Quarry – and to see the hills in plain opposition. In fact, the hills are a wasteland of peat bogs so degraded that every year they issue more than half a million tonnes of carbon dioxide, an act of despoliation in scale and impact immeasurably greater than all of those other industries combined.

When the Foot and Mouth crisis came to an end, the farming industry was reinstated, traumatized but essentially the same. New, disorientated flocks arrived on these hills. The numberless saplings disappeared. Even for somebody like myself, for whom sheep-farming is the basic condition, you couldn't help but wonder why – why support remained so rigid, even for the most remote, the most marginal farms. After all, then as now, farming in Wales is a political choice; basic payments provided by the government constitute 84 per cent of a typical farm income. At the time, though there were many conversations, the answer that struck me most forcefully came from a book, *Where We Belong*, a collection of reflections on life in the Brecon Beacons. Here Matthew Williams, a farmer from Cantref, writes: 'It is certain that without financial aid the hill sheep industry and the way of life that accompanies it would disappear, and Cantref would no longer be economically viable. It would become a wilderness.'

Words which, for me, in subsequent years, have become entangled with lines from 'Borderland', one of my favourite of Chris Meredith's poems:

> You'll find a *ffin** inside each definition.
> We see what is when we see what it's not:
> edges are where meanings happen ...

These upland farms comprise the edges: the edges of the habitable ground, and so the edges of our society. True, it is possible to make too much of farms that have been in the same family for many generations – to see only continuity, to overlook the fights between siblings, the absences of direct succession, the farmers who never wished to be farmers and lost truer selves to the pressures of history. All the same, there is this basic fact: the uplands of Wales were cleared of their wildwood between approximately 4400 and 2300 BC, and since then, excepting Foot and Mouth, they have been grazed by sheep or cattle. If the legend of Llyn y Fan Fach can be said to remember a threat that would date perhaps from 700 BC, then it hardly seems a stretch to imagine that these isolated, hereditary communities might remember

---

* *Ffin* is the Welsh for *border*. It occurs inside *diffiniaid*, which means definition, and in *Capel y Ffin*, a place in the Black Mountains. (Christopher Meredith's note)

the wilderness as a fundamental to resist at any cost. After all, the wilderness comprised a threat for millennia. And if Chris Meredith is right, if the edges reveal the character of the whole, it follows that this attitude revealed in the hills might belong to our culture more widely: an essential, affective but forgotten component of our relationship to the natural world.

Regardless. Turn your back on Fan Brycheiniog. Scramble the few yards over these earthworks until you are able to see to the north. Look past the narrow Gwydderig Valley, where the A40 burrows through the overhanging woodland, to the grey expanse and the black plantations of the next hill, Mynydd Epynt, scene of the pyres in 2001. There, in 1939, 219 people on fifty-four farms were given three months to leave their homes and not a penny in compensation. Their 16,000 hectares of upland grazing were turned into a military training area – destroying a largely Welsh-speaking community.

There have been many such clearances in Wales, some of them in living memory – and this is only one of the ways in which the country is being encroached. The fear described by the farmer Matthew Williams – the old Welsh terror of annihilation, culturally, linguistically – this is no atavistic quirk.

Indeed, it may never have been more valid.

*

'Did you ever read Wythnos yng Nghymru Fydd?' *asks Judith Thornton. 'The Islwyn Ffowc Elis novel?'*

Dr Thornton is Low Carbon Manager at the Institute of Biology, Environmental and Rural Sciences, Aberystwyth University.

We are talking on Zoom in March 2021.

I confess that my Welsh would not be up to such a task – though I know it is something of a science-fiction classic. (In fact, just after this conversation it was published in English translation.)

'*It was sort of a manifesto,*' Judith says, '*for what the future of Wales could be. It painted two pictures. One was thriving local economies, thriving language and culture. And the alternative was the County of Western England – that was the phrase that was used. And that's my concern: if we don't engage with how to create the future we want in Wales, we are really at risk of becoming the County of Western England. For me, in our university department, I think we would be doing a huge disservice to our local communities if we weren't willing to have discussions about the challenges faced by farming. The trusted, critical friend role is one that we have built up over a hundred years of existence. If anybody is going to be able to take farmers and the NFU and FUW [National Farmers' Union and Farmers' Union of Wales] by the hand and lead them towards a solution, it's us. I mean, this is a taboo subject, but the Welsh government aren't doing it, and if we don't talk about it, it would feel . . . quite dishonest, really.*'

'*What are the challenges, then?*' I ask. '*Can you spell them out?*'

'*Well, it's quite instructive to look at the Climate Change Committee's advice to Wales. Basically, the Welsh government asked for advice on meeting their 2050 net-zero target, and the CCC replied by saying that, under our Balanced Pathway, this is what we think the land use would look like by 2030, 2035, 2040, all the way through. To start with, at a simple level, it would require a 30 per cent reduction in rough grassland by 2030. What does that mean, in terms of livestock? Largely, it means getting the sheep off the uplands. And the way of doing that is to pay farmers for carbon sequestration and pay them for peat restoration and restoration of biodiversity on upland heather. But . . . Just getting the sheep off the uplands is a major cultural shift, not to mention the landscape shift.*'

'*Yes . . .*' I say. '*Then, what, you'd be looking at extensive spruce plantations as well?*'

'Not so much right in the uplands. It's pretty important not to be putting forestry on peat. The important thing with any peat soil is to prevent it losing more peat, because that's causing huge emissions, and we need to slow those down, stop them and potentially start reaccumulating peat wherever we can. Which means blocking up drainage ditches and actively rewetting areas in order to help ecosystems regenerate.'

'And they wouldn't just cover with trees, of themselves?' I ask, remembering the saplings during Foot and Mouth.

'There are some places,' Judith says, 'where, if you just put a fence around it, it will turn back into woodland. But we've got an upland research farm at Pwllpeiran, just above Aberystwyth, with plots of land that we've deliberately just left, having fenced the sheep off for twenty years, and they look pretty much the same as they did. So it's not at all predictable what landscapes end up looking like, once you've left them to their own devices ... Actually, I don't think it's wise to have a big reforest-the-uplands plan. You could have some natural regeneration, maybe. But if you let everything turn to forest then you've lost all your semi-natural grassland, for example. So there is still a chopping-things-down job to be done, to maintain that mosaic of habitats.'

'OK ...' I search through my notes. 'But the CCC have said that we need "43,000 hectares of new mixed woodland" by 2030, "rising to 180,000 hectares by 2050". That's an area almost the size of Breconshire ... If we can't plant on the uplands because of the peat, then presumably we will have to plant on productive farmland?'

'Well,' says Judith, 'in terms of the CCC's scenario, it's handy to split things into three zones, rather than two. The uplands are for carbon and biodiversity – restoration of blanket bog, restoration of heather – and along the way you'll probably discover that this has beneficial impacts in terms of flooding, so other ecosystem services as well. *The lowlands are for intensive agricultural production. And then we have this middle ground, verging into the uplands, which is where you'd see the productive forestry ... It would be great if the Welsh government took on the CCC's advice on land use as a challenge. Most of the evidence suggests that "land-sparing" – intensifying agricultural production in some areas while preserving biodiversity as a clear and distinct goal in other areas – maximizes benefits to both production and ecosystems. Instead, the Welsh government seems to be going down the route of "land-sharing" – that is, the idea that agricultural production and ecosystem benefits can be integrated on the same parcel of land. That's seen as less threatening by the farming community but it remains to be seen if it will deliver for the environment.'*

'And how would this – how would you put it? – how would this lead to a cultural collapse? What would be the trigger?'

'The subsidy regime,' Judith says, simply. 'When the regime changes to support other activities, when the livestock start dis-appearing – though, unfortunately, the Welsh government don't have a clear plan on what they intend those subsidies to look like in the future. I mean, will there be agricultural subsidies in ten years' time? I don't know. I don't know ... I do see the subsidy regime as an opportunity to do something sensible. When you've got an upland farmer who, you know, 80 per cent of your income comes from subsidy, well, what on earth are we doing? You could stay in bed, couldn't you, for 80 per cent of your income? But then, if we weren't in this situation, I couldn't see us getting to the point of having a conversation about methane.'

Methane, of course, is a greenhouse gas more than eighty times more powerful than carbon dioxide over a twenty-year period. Among its main sources are the digestive processes of cattle, sheep and other ruminants.

'So the subsidy regime changes and –?'

'Imagine you're a heating engineer, and that's the profession you've chosen, and someone comes along and says now you've got to be a carpenter, you'd be like, hang on a minute ... How dare you? Farmers provide us with food, and that's why they're getting out of bed every day, and to be told that actually you need to provide fibre or timber products or –'

'But surely something like that has to happen – for peat restoration or –?'

'Yes, but if you're a farmer, is that what you want to do? Or are you just going to sell up to a forestry company? And it's an ageing population, isn't it? The average Welsh farmer is well over sixty. If I was a farmer and I was getting on a bit, I'd think, well, maybe I should retire now and just sell my farm, because I don't see a future for it. And that's the point at which all the other things step in. That's why I'm so keen for farming to undergo a managed and strategic contraction, because if we get uncoordinated, catastrophic collapse, then loads of farms will go out of business and all those farms will get bought up. It's hugely concerning. Companies will be buying up land and claiming huge carbon drawdown subsidies, to allow polluting industries to continue elsewhere. And then you've got your eco-colonialists, a whole bunch of rewilding projects: people wanting to impose their vision on Wales without having any understanding of the local context. Then there'll be other people trying to turn everything into pheasant shoots and deer-coursing, like Scottish estates: playground-for-the-English types. And all of those, culturally, are really catastrophic.'

For a moment, Judith and I are looking at one another, each with our own bits of Wales around us. I find myself thinking of Banwen Colliery, of Chris and the hilltop estates of Tredegar – of the misery, the devastation caused by an industry's collapse.

'You mentioned methane,' I say, eventually. 'If you look at what

the NFU, for example, has to say about food additives to reduce
methane emissions from livestock – would such things change the
picture at all?'

'Undoubtedly, we can farm animals much more efficiently,' she
says. 'And it's definitely the case that there are food additives on
the cusp of availability which will significantly decrease methane
emissions. But it's also fair to say that, even if we had very high
levels of uptake of the current innovations, there's a huge gap
between what is achievable with current innovation and where
we need to get to. To date, most of these things work extremely
well in test tubes, and then ... You start off saying, that's great,
that'll cause an 80 per cent decrease in methane production by
the ruminant. But by the time it actually gets to the levels that are
then added in feed and demonstrated in a large trial you tend to
be down to single-digit improvements ... You have to ask yourself:
let's say that a food additive leads to a 10 per cent reduction in
emissions, isn't it easier just to have fewer ruminants in the first
place?*

'In the end, I think, we're going to have a few rich people eating
prime, 100 per cent Welsh Black steak and most of the rest of us
then choose between whether we want vegetables that are made
to look and taste like meat, or whether we want vegetables.'*

She pauses a moment, sighs distinctly. 'Shall we have a positive
five minutes?'*

'Oh yes,' I say, 'by all means.'*

'One of the positive visions for the future, for me, is that by
2050 we are not going to be making stuff out of fossil fuels. At the
moment we are in a fossil-fuel-based economy. Before we had oil
and gas, we used to be in an economy based on plants and natural
materials, and in the future we need to be there again. And not
just for energy, but for all of the stuff: that plastic bottle you've
just had a swig out of, the pen that you've got in your hand, your*

*clothing, everything – all of our stuff is going to need to be made
out of natural materials. And where is the feedstock for all of this
going to come from? It's going to come from rural areas. It's going
to come from the green and pleasant land of mid-Wales. So we're
going to be the ones who are growing grass to feed to biorefineries
to make into plastic bags. You can still be a farmer who grows
grass, you just won't have anything with four legs eating it. The
farmers of Wales are going to be the ones who are growing the
specialist form of plant that turns out to have a new pharmaceut-
ical product in it. We're going to be the ones who are growing the
plant-based proteins. And, at the same time, if you look at the
CCC's Pathway in terms of its negative emissions technologies,
almost all of their solutions have an extremely important role
for farmers and farming. We can't have biomass energy without
land to grow the biomass on. We can't have biochar [a carbon-
rich, charcoal-like substance] incorporation into land without the
land. We can't have peatland restoration without the people who
own the peatland being willing to restore. So, in the same way
that the South Wales Valleys fuelled the Industrial Revolution by
providing the feedstocks for it, it could be that rural areas will provide the goods for the future economy. At the moment we provide
food, and in the future we need to provide everything else as well.'*

*

Weaving down the west end of Mynydd Bach Trecastell,
the first you see of Hafod Fawr – the first of the houses of
Carmarthenshire – is fallen slates, a bare stone wall, a window
teetering out of its socket. The front of the house looks a little less
derelict, having a serviceable door and windows, but the roof
here too is smothered in moss, while the ancient whitewash is
streaked brown-green where the gutter is broken and sags from
its brackets. A Ford Ka, the cheapest of vehicles, is parked just

inside the yard. Next to the tin-and-concrete shed is a Massey
Ferguson 2640: a desirable tractor when I was a child, all of
forty years ago. That smell of fleece and damp and dung. This
farm feels so basically familiar. When I was a child, our neighbours across the valley were a pair of grizzled and tooth-short
brothers, plus their tiny mother in her pale-blue housecoat.
They had buildings on the edge of ruin. Their cattle were so
immersed in mud and manure that all movement was close to
impossible. It was common enough at that time, in Radnorshire,
for a family to have left most of their house to the weather, to
be living in only a couple of rooms, in a stench that was almost
solid. And when, in my early thirties, I lived near Rhayader in
the Cambrian Mountains, the situation could be even worse.
One neighbour had given up his house altogether. You could
see how, in one part, the rafters had fallen, how he had moved
into a final room, patching its windows with plastic bags, and
then, when this room could no longer be salvaged, he had moved
into a succession of vans, each one smaller than the last, all of
them rotting round the edges of the yard. About a year after I
arrived, he was injured by a cow, and then died of gangrene in
Aberystwyth Hospital.

Rural poverty. Not an issue given much public notice.

So much depends on places like this: this small, working farm
among its high, wet fields, its hedges sprouted into spindly trees,
its beeches and sycamores and rusting sheds and old machinery in shoulder-deep nettles. First in importance is always the
language. The Welsh-speaking tracts of the north and west are
secured by farms in hereditary ownership, most of them on
Severely Disadvantaged Land, all of them vulnerable to the risks
inherent in any contraction of the livestock industry. But beyond
the language there is everything else. Just this name, Hafod
Fawr, remembers the traditional system of transhumance – of

hafod (summer upland holding) and *hendre* (permanent low-land holding). This method of farming may now have been reduced to a basic, seasonal movement of stock, but it dates at least from the Middle Ages, and probably very long before.

The quiet fragility of it all, of everything that makes Wales distinct; it could all go without notice, just as our flocks of starlings have dwindled, just as the house martins have left our eaves, just as on Mynydd Illtyd, not twenty years ago, there used to be curlews, lapwings, redshanks – and now there are only the aeroplanes.

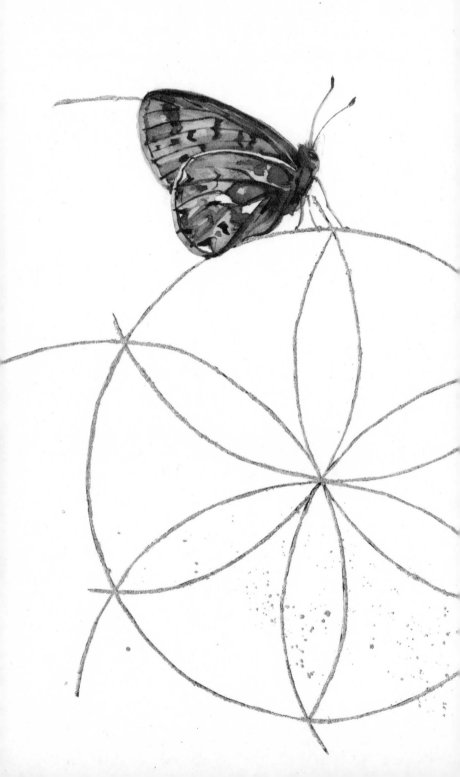

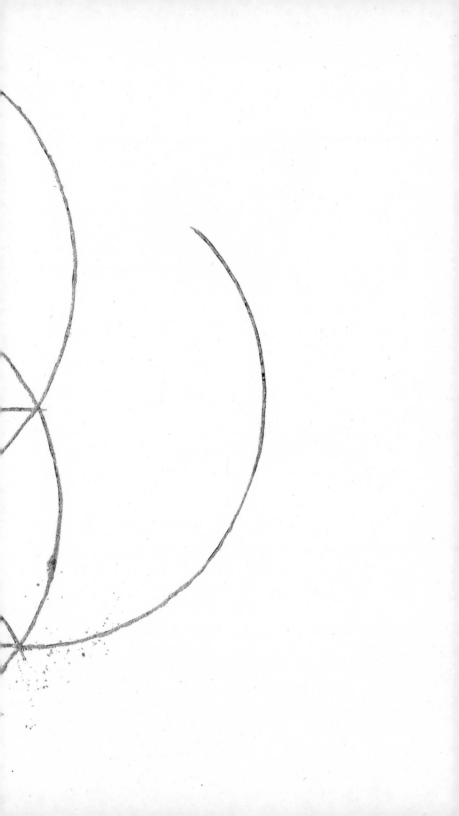

4

Llandovery to Cockshead Wood

14 September 2020

The West End Café, on Broad Street in Llandovery, is usually a mass of bikers: those fearsome, anonymous figures who scream in packs along the A40, and then come here to remove their helmets and reveal themselves as less Johnny Strabler, more retired solicitor from Stoke-on-Trent. Today the place is close to deserted. There is only the girl in the plastic visor who fills my mug at the stainless-steel counter. There are only the Poles at one of the tables, talking softly over bacon sandwiches – their voices putting me in mind of Anna, who worked for Charlie for several years but, with the pandemic having finished for the café, has just this weekend collected her possessions and driven back to her mother near Wrocław.

I carry my tea through the blazing morning, to a wrought-iron bench in Market Square.

The lane is steep, beneath Hafod Fawr. In the eighteenth century, before the valley road was built, teams of oxen were required to haul the coaches up the slope on to that track over

Mynydd Bach Trecastell. Often, as you make the descent, you are able to see this entire *ystrad*, this generous, flat-bottomed valley, its mosaic of fields and billowing woods deep and green against the bare, brown backs of Mynydd Mallaen and Esgair Ferchon. The town itself, on its leg of ground between the Tywi and the Brân, might almost be Neath again. Everything suggests a decent living: the big metal roofs of the industrial estates; the rugby fields and Gothic halls of the independent school; the grand, grey church, Llanfair-ar-y-Bryn, assembled from the ruins of Alabum Fort. You would not know that, in this square of half-barrels brimming with flowers, of Georgian buildings salmon-pink, scarlet, ochre and marine-blue, only two of the six shops remain in business – and of those one sells novelty plaques saying things like 'It's always prosecco o'clock'.

Early one Monday, perhaps ten years ago, Rocket and I were stacking boards in the dry shed at my father's sawmill. Rocket – his given name is Paul – is an industrious, red-headed man with a permanent look of involved reflection. He grew up on a pig farm in Letton, three or four miles into England, though his family comes from the hills near Knucklas, about a mile on the Welsh side of the border. There, every Sunday, they all would assemble – uncles, sisters, grandmothers, cousins – to sit around a very large table and, so far as I could gather, insult one another. Here, every Monday, I would ask after the weekend and Rocket would say something of his Sunday dinner, at which anything seemed to be fair ammunition: your new car, that sodden field, that indiscretion at the YFC disco back in 1982.

'Does anyone,' I asked this once, 'ever bring up Wales and England?'

Rocket looked less reflective than baffled at the question. 'They never have,' he said.

At the time, partly to help with a novel, I was talking to a number of elderly farmers around Radnorshire and Breconshire, and I started to ask what the border meant to them.

'I don't bother much about it,' said Walter Price of Rhulen.

'It is never mentioned,' said Matthew Price of Hundred House.

'Well, it's all a bloody laugh,' said Robert Tyler of Llandeilo Graban.

The Welsh–English border, as it is normally construed, as it was defined by the 1536 Act of Union, runs for some 250 miles between the estuaries of the Dee and the Severn. It twists and wanders and, by and large, outside of local government and some middling novels, nobody pays it very much attention. It is true that the devolution of health services to Wales has given the border a fresh significance, particularly with Covid-19. For months my mother could not see her brother, since that would have been to cross the Dulas Brook. But, from a local point of view, it has merely proved what we already knew: the border is an arbitrary line, straddled by families, farms and towns.

This can lead you to wonder if, in fact, the border ought to have been drawn somewhere else. It is an interesting question with various answers. The first is that, in all justice, the border ought to be the North Sea. Originally, as the argument goes, Great Britain belonged to the Celtic Britons, speakers of the Brittonic language which would eventually evolve into Welsh. When the Anglo-Saxons invaded, spreading inland from the south and east, containing the last of the Brittonic-speaking tribes in the mountainous north and west, they were stealing the birthright of the people of Wales. There are some issues with this analysis. One is that the Brittonic-speaking tribes had themselves overcome an earlier people. Another is that all of these groups, over centuries and millennia, appear to have intermarried. Even in Wales the most long-standing families have about 30 per cent Anglo-Saxon ancestry, as opposed to the 44 per cent Anglo-Saxon ancestry of their equivalents in East Anglia. All the same, it is a view with heft for all red-blooded nationalists – and it does have the merit of relative simplicity.

The closer you come to the border in law, the more complex the picture becomes. In the south, you could make a case that Ergyng, the former Welsh kingdom mostly located in modern Herefordshire, should really be a part of Wales. Parts of Herefordshire, after all, remained Welsh-speaking well into the eighteenth century – by which time Radnorshire basically spoke English. And if Ergyng were to be included, then Pengwern in Shropshire, once a part of the Kingdom of Powys, would surely have to be included too. On the other hand, Monmouthshire, the historic county, was depicted as English on OS maps as recently as the 1960s.

Spend some time at Crickadarn Castle, high in the hills of Breconshire, and you may start to wonder at its D-shaped earth-works – at the way that they look towards the river. The reason is that, in the twelfth and thirteenth centuries, the Welsh held the east bank of the Wye Valley while the Normans held the west.

The border was the other way around. And a good seven miles from Offa's Dyke, which was erected by the Mercians 400 years earlier to bring a resolution to this problem.

Another, more recent conversation with a farmer was in the extreme west of Radnorshire, not twenty miles from Cardigan Bay. One evening in 2016, I went up to Aberglanhirin, a bunga-low with shed and barn, sheltered to the west by a belt of pines but otherwise alone in the upper Elan Valley, where the river follows improbable meanders among the barren Cambrian

Mountains. Robert Hughes sat with his tea in his armchair, the expression on his weather-worn face, half-concealed by his base-ball cap, partly amiable, partly wary in the characteristic way.

His wife, in the kitchen, was smoking a roll-up.

The pendant light in the middle of the ceiling was pulsing with the current of the diesel generator.

'Do you see this as a Welsh place?' I asked. 'Do you see your-selves as Welsh?'

'Welsh, in a way.' Robert gave a soft laugh. 'I'd like to think it, like. But at the same time, we are Radnorshire. You can't say we're really Welsh, are we, like? Radnorshire's classed as an English county in a way, isn't it, like? But then you go up the road half a mile and you're in Cardiganshire then.'

'And that's what you'd call really Welsh?'

'Oh, Cardiganshire's really Welsh.'

'And it's the language that would be the difference?'

'Yeah. Once you go over there … Hey, cat!' He swept a lynx-like creature from his lap. 'I used to have an uncle living down there, about six or seven mile away, and he was Welsh-speaking. His brother, uncles, all the neighbours coming up to help, they're all speaking Welsh. I go down there and I'm the odd one out, like. You're just sitting there, listening. Grin and bear it and just listen!'

Robert, of course, has a singular perspective. As a farmer, he rarely gets to spend the time elsewhere that can help to see a cultural consonance in Wales. 'You go to Breconshire,' he said at one point, 'it's the difference like a foreign land.' All the same, you can see how, for him, those western slopes of the Cambrian Mountains – a presence almost since I left Llandovery – could seem to be the real border.

*

It has gone two o'clock in the afternoon when, in a narrow valley buried in woodland, a winding wheel reveals itself, orange among the shining leaves. Next comes a cluster of green-blue sheds. Then the padlocked gate of a large, empty car park, its sign spelling out the latest Covid-19 restrictions. Hard though it is to imagine now, it was only in the 1840s that a geologist named Sir Warington Wilkinson Smyth chanced upon Dolaucothi Gold Mine, which locally had been quite forgotten. From my point of view this is a place of legend. I must have been seven when a friend of my brother Ol came here on a day trip with his parents, returning with tales of the gleaming nuggets you could simply collect from the floors of the tunnels. From a Roman point of view, it was the meat in the meal. As the only gold mine in Roman Britain, it must have been a deciding factor when Tacitus, in AD 98, concluded that the province 'produces gold and silver and other metals: conquest is worthwhile'. The achievements of the Romans here, as is always the way with the Romans, are still enough to bend the mind. Between the late first and the late fourth centuries they built reservoirs, leats and aqueducts, channelling 2 million gallons of water a day into the rock faces holding the gold-bearing quartz; they used water-wheels in sequence for draining and enormous, water-powered trip hammers to crush the ore against a rock which came to be known as Carreg Pumsaint – the hammers' indentations being later ascribed to the heads of five saints sheltering from a storm sent upon them by an evil sorcerer.

Each tonne of ore produced a quantity of gold about the size of a sugar cube.

Each load of ingots, in military convoy, was carried south along Sarn Helen – usually, to the Imperial Mint at Lyons.

*

The words 'Sarn Helen' return to the map a mile or so north of the village of Pumsaint, following a long, straight lane without the slightest shade from the sun. With them, the landscape of the past five hours – contours charted by tree-rich hedgerows, by tiny, wet and tucked-away dingles and hills whose turf is the barest skin – subsides and then disappears. In its place is nothing much. The Cambrian Mountains remain in the east, pale and stark in the stark-blue sky: naked tops and pits of shadow. But these fields, green and sloping moderately, these hedges trimmed into featureless boxes, the murky water of the River Twrch, this farm where a dog is barking, conducting an argument with its own echo – these are simply and tirelessly dull.

My shadow drags across the tarmac.

My sweat drips from alternating elbows.

One issue with walking the length of Wales is that the further you go from home the harder it becomes to get back. There is no bus service even from Llandovery to Brecon, a thirty-five-minute drive along a main road. Enter these lanes to their north and west and public transport is all but non-existent. Ideally, of course, I would have packed my things and walked to Caerhun in a single leg, but in practice, just to find three days to try to continue as far as Machynlleth has been an industrial operation. Which means I must do my walking now, plagued by flies with metallic backs and dreams about a shop with rows of fridges crammed with cold and sugar-rich drinks. Which means I have a rucksack stuffed to the neck with pots of food and bottles of water, adding its awkward, sweat-soaked bulk to a sun that might have been organized: a specific taunt to all of those parents whose few days of summer holiday involved a tent in Pembrokeshire in the now-customary August monsoon.

As it will transpire, going mostly unremarked, this is the hottest September since records began – Europe-wide, by 0.2°C.

The River Twrch feeds under the lane.

Of the legends of Wales, the wildest, surely, has to be 'How Culhwch Won Olwen' – including, as it does, Twrch Trwyth. This is a king transformed by God for his sins into a magical, ferocious boar, who holds between his ears the scissors, comb and razor required to trim the hair of the Chief of the Giants. The hunt of Twrch Trwyth involves King Arthur – this is, in fact, his earliest romance – pursuing the boar and his seven fearsome piglets from Ireland to Porth Clais near St David's and from there, with much slaughter and laying waste to kingdoms, across South Wales and down into Cornwall, where he is driven finally into the sea. At a certain point in the chase, however, Twrch Trwyth and two of his offspring, Grugyn Gwrych Eraint and Llwydog Gofyniad, are cornered close to Llyn y Fan Fawr, one of the two lakes beneath Fan Brycheiniog. Here the three are parted by Arthur's hounds and huntsmen, and Grugyn, who would seem to have a point when he says that 'God has done us enough harm by shaping us in this image, without you too coming to fight against us', escapes north towards Aberystwyth, 'wreak[ing] the greatest havoc possible'.

There are various places in Wales said to remember the hunt of Twrch Trwyth – among them another River Twrch (the name means 'boar'), this one rising to the south of Fan Brycheiniog to join the Tawe at Ystalyfera. Perhaps, following the Roman road, it was this way that Grugyn fled for his last stand near Llanilar. Perhaps this irrelevant thread of a river now wandering off to the local sewage works could provide another example. It is a thought to fit the black of my mood: an enormous, frenzied boar, his terrible bristles 'like wings of silver', hurtling north along this valley, upturning everything that stands in his path.

At the southern end of Ffarmers, a bungalow doubles as a plant hire company. It looks from an eminence over its lawns, where a Husqvarna Automower is maintaining a quarter-inch of grass. In the village itself are further bungalows, each with its Volvo V60 or Suzuki Vitara parked on a tongue of broiling tarmac, each with its corner of quarter-inch grass. The place feels dystopian. In all of the village there is no one to be seen, Welsh-speaking or otherwise. There are only these robot mowers – I see three at work, all told – creeping carefully around their gardens, ensuring an aesthetic for no one to appreciate. In a country where one in six species of all wildlife, plants and fungi is threatened with imminent national extinction, their job is kill any weed or flower that might potentially foster life.

*

'Curlew is a good example,' says Paul Sinnadurai. 'People always used to assume that curlew were a natural indicator of nice wet grassland with good arable margins: areas where the chicks and the adults would feed. Then people were just scratching their heads, thinking, where have they gone? Well, obviously there'll be reasons. Their foraging habitat has disappeared. They haven't got enough places or enough security to rear their chicks. The places where they winter on the coast have been interrupted. And if any population goes through a critical low threshold, then it crashes and simply doesn't return.'

Dr Sinnadurai FCIEEM is Senior Ecologist for the Brecon Beacons National Park Authority and an Honorary Research Fellow at Cardiff University. (He is talking to me on his own behalf.) It is October 2021 and, of all things, we are sitting in the same room: upstairs in The Hours Café in Brecon, with a table, tea and cake between us and, across the road, through a wonky sash window, a tile shop and the former town library – its pale-grey concrete half-consumed by ivy.

'I think,' I say, 'that curlew are fledging fewer than half of the chicks that they'd need to maintain a population?'

'Yes,' says Paul. 'And it's probably requiring every effort from the RSPB and others even to maintain that.'

'So the outlook for curlew is probably local extinction?'

'At the moment. I submit records when I hear them. I very rarely see them these days, though I did hear them flying over the house in the springtime so they must be somewhere in the Usk Valley.'

'What I've been told is that they are returning, nesting, but that the young do not survive, so pairs are slowly disappearing as time goes on?'

'Yes. Yes, that's right. Happily, the RSPB has identified the Usk Valley as one of the twelve important curlew areas across Wales, so the hope is to build back with that over the long term. But there are so many other examples. The red squirrel is another. During my life as an ecologist, I've seen these species just disappear. I've seen a catastrophic decline in so many species, which feels like a failure on my part. My profession hasn't done enough, hasn't found a way to win the argument about safeguarding areas beyond the boundaries of the SSSIs [Sites of Special Scientific Interest].

'The thing is: even with the few resources that have been thrown at it, the nature conservation system has always worked. SSSIs have always worked, but there's never been enough of them and they were never big enough, and they were always identified on marginal land anyway. What we have, largely, are Sites designated on bits that couldn't be cultivated or can't be built on. These were never the most productive parts of the farmed environment, and yet we've called them our jewels in the crown. Well, we've taken the jewels in the crown for ourselves, though we've changed them so much that they're not recognizable as that any more.

We've marginalized wildlife. We've pushed it on to these fragments of land, and they just aren't functioning. We've asked too
much of them. And all the while, my profession has been saying,
yes, but it's the wider countryside that we really need to focus on.
We've always been saying, why can't we make the landscape work?
Why can't we recover ecological integrity, ecological function?'

Paul speaks softly, rapidly. Though his words are those of a scientist, their delivery has much the same precision as his posture.
Formerly, he was a ballet dancer – he has performed with the
Bavarian State Ballet and the London City Ballet – and he retains
that poise, that verticality.

He pauses, takes a sip of tea.

'And,' I say, 'I assume this decline applies across the board? I
think, say, of the phosphate levels in the Usk and the Wye, of that
pressure on fish and invertebrates . . .'

'Yes,' Paul nods. 'To take the area I'm probably most familiar
with. For my PhD, I studied the riparian carabid beetles on the
exposed river shingles on the River Usk. What we were looking
for were the classic signs of a species that can cope with catastrophic drought, because these areas can be very dry, and then
catastrophic flooding when they get flooded, which is a cycle
that these species and groups have evolved to live in. But these
gravels didn't flood for the entirety of those three years, so I didn't
get to observe that at all. What I got to observe was, if you like,
their terrestrialization as the gravels dried out and as vegeta-
tion encroached, and the areas that the beetles were viable for
diminished. And the reason that was happening was changing
meteorological patterns. There was a drought for three years. But
then the River Usk is also heavily abstracted for water . . . I mean,
everything that we're trying to deal with is anthropogenic. None
of these things are natural.'

A young woman has emerged from the top of the stairs, trying

*at once to carry a cup of coffee and to calm the baby yowling on
her chest. She sends a tight, tired smile across the room, sets her
cup on an empty table and starts a soothing, shuffling dance.*

'So ... there's agriculture.' I lean forward a little to be heard.
'And water abstraction. What are the other main pressures?'

'Urbanization,' says Paul. 'Afforestation. Energy generation.
You know,' he gives the quick and empty laugh usual to these
conversations, 'where are we going to get our energy supplies
from in the future? It's almost an abstract concept because every
decision we make is a hydrocarbon-supported decision. The
distances we travel. The towns we live in and the way they've
been built – especially as they're designed nowadays – they're
designed for the internal combustion engine. Our agricultural
sector, that has been a response to food demand, which has
been driven by fossil-fuel-supported economies, societies and
population growth – which has improved our quality of life,
but has also allowed us to exploit systems at an exponential
rate ... And now the idea is that we have electric vehicles that
allow us to make exactly the same decisions and to live our lives
in exactly the same way and be equally exploitative and travel
equally far. But the problems are so fundamental. For example,
as fossil fuels are removed from the equation, that is going to
mean an end to bitumen and asphalt. If we can't surface our
roads, what are we even going to put these vehicles on in the
future? We're not digging deep enough in our thinking. We're not
asking hard enough questions about ourselves, about whether
any of this is really achievable over the long term. It's like we've
all got this blooming great tyrannosaurus rex by the tail and
none of us dare let go because we don't know what's going to
bite us where ...'

*The baby, abruptly, has fallen quiet; it makes our laughter seem
unnaturally loud. At the bottom of Ship Street the lights turn*

green, and the endless, rumbling line of vehicles creeps down the hill towards the Usk Bridge.

'And,' I say, 'as you know, in not daring to let go we're looking at temperature rises of 3°C or more. I mean, what are the implications for biodiversity under those kinds of climatic and temperature changes?'

'Well,' says Paul, 'the way it's classically presented is that you're looking at a shifting climate envelope – whether that's an altitudinal or a latitudinal shift – and that's only going to work if the various species have got places to move to. The problem we come up against is that they may well have been able to do that in the past, over tens of thousands of years, when the landscape wasn't occupied by a very dominant species. Now they're going to have to make this shift in maybe fifty, a hundred years, when that landscape has been completely changed and isn't suitable for them. And that's asking a huge amount because it requires people to make it possible, and most people are never going to be involved with this. They're just going to be getting on with their lives. They're not going to be thinking: as well as taking my children to school, and then going shopping, and then going to work, how do I make sure a pearl-bordered fritillary butterfly can move fifty miles over the next ten years? You know, it's abstract. It's not within their ken. So we really need to find a new societal way of thinking about these things.'

'Do you recognize the idea of the sixth mass extinction?' I ask, this being a term often used to describe our predicament. Previous mass extinction events include the Cretaceous–Paleogene, which saw the end of the non-avian dinosaurs. 'Do you think it's too early to talk in those terms?'

'No, I think it's pretty sure. I'm very convinced by the Anthropocene arguments ...' He pauses a moment, knits his fingers. 'Back in 2018, there was a conference involving the

British Ecological Society, the Chartered Institute of Ecology and Environmental Management and the conservation agencies of Britain, and Professor Ian Boyd was one of the keynote speakers. He was DEFRA's Chief Scientist at the time. Ian came in and basically said, "We need disruptive change. It's got to happen."'

'Meaning?'

'Meaning we need to shake up everything, and there needs to be a revolution. Not evolution but a revolution, because we need to save nature by 2030 or it's game over. That's what he was saying, and that was only twelve years out when he said it, and now it's that much closer again, and I still don't see the signs. I still don't see the land designations – the areas outside the reserves and the National Parks – that enable people to change their behaviour and bring nature recovery into their lives.'

'And by "game over" you mean?'

'He was talking about critical thresholds, beyond which things just can't recover.'

The baby has resumed his howling.

The glass and concrete of the building opposite amplifies the roar of a tractor.

'Maybe,' I say, 'this is a good time to talk about ecosystem services? I mean, what is it that ecosystems do for us, as people?'

'OK.' Paul finishes his tea, sits back. 'Let's start at the top of the hill and work our way downwards. At the top of the hill, in this part of Wales, we've got plateaus of deep peat, which keep historic, atmospheric carbon underground – or they do where they're intact. They're also crucial for flood regulation and potentially can function like water storage batteries for micro-hydrogeneration. So there are three services straight away. Where we've got homesteads and farmsteads, they'll have been using wells or surface water in order to establish a water system. Go back through Brecon's history and we had two or three watermills

just on the River Honddu. So: energy from water, flood manage-
ment, drinking water, irrigation water ... Then we could look
at trees. We only have about 13 per cent tree cover in Britain
overall, so we've largely lost trees as a timber supply and as a
forage, a fodder crop for browsing livestock. But we could talk
about carbon sequestration there as well. And then, of course,
there's food production. Insect pollination throws up some really
interesting challenges, because that requires species-rich pasture,
hay meadow, species-rich verges, hedge banks and so on. But do
we foster that kind of environment in a mechanistic sort of a way,
mixing and matching with how we put trees back into the land-
scape? Which areas do we re-wet? And then, we have what people
call "special qualities": the tranquillity, the beauty, the colours, the
spiritual renewal ...'

'But, essentially,' I say, 'these are "services" on which humans
absolutely depend?'

'Oh gosh, yes.'

'So,' I say, 'I'm sort of losing faith in this question, but what do
you think might be the solution?'

'I think,' Paul says, 'the solutions lie in the whole thing around
local supply chains, living locally, thinking locally, making local
areas more self-sufficient, providing greater opportunity to live
your life locally. We need to ramp up what we now call nature
recovery as much as we can, wherever and whenever we can. And
we don't need to be too fussy about it. Nature needs to be able to
recover everywhere. We can have, if you like, hotspots for nature
and hotspots for food production, but the nature areas need to be
really natural and the food production areas need to be as tech-
nically advanced as they possibly can be, while allowing nature
to thrive there as well. And then we need to sit and watch what
happens. We need to establish huge monitoring and surveillance
programmes because monitoring and surveillance are, and always

have been, the poor relation in nature conservation work because they're resource-intensive. Anyone who's got a piece of garden, or a window sill, can be part of the solution. With wild flowers, in terms of pollinators, you can do an awful lot. If you've got some outdoor space, you can easily divide it into 10 per cent seasonal fruit or veg, and then you can put another 10 per cent to habitat. Goodness me, it's much less labour-intensive to manage for wildlife than it is even to maintain a lawn. And let's get everyone recording and generating data. Let's help my profession to do that, because I tend to think, well, if my profession's time hasn't come now, then when the hell is it going to come?'

*

Slowly, slowly the land begins to gather, the heat to subside with the afternoon. The fields grow pinched and angular. The lane is strewn for periods with beech mast, the first-falling leaves of the oaks, the red-yellow leaves of a few horse chestnuts, which, as ever, are weeks ahead. Ahead, where it seems that the hills converge, scratched by screes and cut by cliffs, a paraglider hangs entirely motionless. It appears to have been nailed to the sky. It remains in its place for an hour and more, while a microlight closes, circles to check, then buzzes away over Cardiganshire, while the tight lane climbs past a final farm of elderly tractor and rusting roofs – into an openness where stone walls crumple, where a rank of beeches remembers the winds, where a second paraglider launches from a crag. Look down and you look across whirling crows and ravens, which pass then roll on their backs and give out their cough-like call. In the valley, the farms and the cottages are huddled among trees in the angling light; they seem suddenly vulnerable, with the hills around so hard and bare.

Careg y Bwci, a long grey monolith, lies sunk into a

pronounced rise between Pant-têg and Esgair Fraith. Its site, according to a sign, is likely to have been both a Bronze Age barrow, perhaps surrounded by a stone circle, and a Roman watch tower and signal station. Its views seem scarcely feasible. The Cambrian Mountains still govern in the east, but in the west are the Preseli Hills, swelling softly from the Pembrokeshire plain, their shapes discovered by scraps of shadow. In the south-east are Fan Brycheiniog and Fan Frynych, whose face I crossed with Chris Meredith. Forty miles away, in the north, the peak of Cadair Idris resembles a volcano.

Suddenly all is vulnerability. Wales: you could just blot it out with your thumb. It feels that small, that threatened. And this is no black, passing mood. The thought that comes has come to me daily, probably for half my life. To me, it is the obvious reaction: how do you make the setting of your story convincingly the centre of a fictional world? It is a question to haunt any novelist of Wales, struggling to grow in the English shadow – and one that can rarely have been asked by any novelist of the major cities. Any reader knows that New York is important, while London, if not the seat of global power that it was in the days of Dickens or Conrad, is established as a place of story. Indeed, having once bought a few weeks' work by writing a literary guide to the city – *The Rough Guide to London by the Book* – I can report that it has no quarter, from Bloomsbury to Greenwich, Primrose Hill to Marylebone, without its canonical fictional tradition. Of course, Wales has myriad traditions in tale, poetry and song. It has had many excellent novelists – Arthur Machen and Caradog Prichard, Kate Roberts and Glyn Jones – but still it wants that fictional key. There remains no Great Welsh Novel for reference, no precedent in voice or style such as Scotland, the obvious analogue, can claim in Scott, Hogg, Stevenson, Lewis Grassic Gibbon or Alasdair Gray. The best-known novelists shaped by Wales, Sarah Waters and Philip Pullman, have both built stories on the sure foundations of London's Victorian smogs and spiritualists and places with names like Hangman's Wharf, and have neither, so far as I am aware, set any work here at all.

In a high-school workshop a few years back, I asked a boy why he had set his story of werewolves on Dartmoor, not on the moors around his town. His answer was a scornful laugh.

For fictional centrality, you might read cultural confidence.

And yet, as you look across these sixty-five miles, this more than half of the length of Wales – from Snowdonia to the Brecon Beacons – such concerns can only subside. It is like watching somebody you love in sleep. The glare of the afternoon is gone, and in its place is a tenderness which envelops this whole expanse: these shades of green becoming grey; this giant sky with its high, rippled clouds, which in Radnorshire you used to call 'cruddledy', curdled. The feeling extends even to Sarn Helen: a means of travel that did not rely on hydrocarbons, stretching north along a slowly falling ridge of walls and fences, unhurried sheep and occasional willows and hawthorns and spruces. On Sarn Helen, by and large, the walking is easy. Of course, the well-being of the troops was core to the Roman military strategy. See the legionary baths at Caerleon if you doubt. But when you conduct your own loaded march for twenty-five miles in the burning heat, the gentle descents and the absence of detours can feel like a kindness too.

By six o'clock the sun is low, the sky luminous. There is a rock by the bridge in Llanfair Clydogau apparently intended for a seat; it looks across the narrow River Teifi – its long-armed weeds, its bending willows, its back which might have been drawn tight.

Alongside is a signpost striped like a lighthouse, which says that it is 3½ miles to Lampeter, 3¾ miles to Llanddewi and 1¾ miles to Llangybi. Across the junction the post office is one of two houses, conjoined Victorian twins of staring windows in square grey walls. In its eaves is a globular nest where a couple of house martins, a rarity now, are bearing food to their gaping young. The racket of their nestlings comes and goes with the fighter jets which cut apart the air. An Izusu Trooper passes; a shaggy-headed man gives a nod from the cab. Big blue tractors are rolling home, towing trailer-loads of hay. Their sweet, dusty scent joins the tang of oil and diesel and, faintly, the savour of frying mince – coming, it seems, from the house beside the chapel.

Dogs are yawping distantly.

A magpie passes, pursued by a crow, and I touch my chest in a superstitious gesture called 'emsin' in Radnorshire – the name deriving from the Welsh *ymswyno*, meaning 'to cross yourself'. It is a rare example, in the local English dialect, of a word whose roots are Welsh. A moment then, victorious, the crow returns to strut around a ragged patch of grass among the beds of neatly planted flowers: the deep-red flowers with golden hearts, and the orange bells, and the lilac stars, and the little clusters of pink and white.

One of the problems of being a farmer is that fair weather necessitates work. My father never joined the rest of us on our summer holidays in the Gower. Some friends, a couple I know from Rhayader, set out on honeymoon twenty-five years ago but got no further than Llandrindod Wells before a good hay-making sun came out – which has been their only attempt at a break. This warm, clear evening is all work, all machines. As I make my way up the following hill, I pass a Zetor 6245, the first of the affordable four-wheel-drive tractors, imported from Czechoslovakia in the 1980s. In the next field is a bodged-together JCB, one of those with the huge-windowed cab, except without the backhoe or the stabilizer legs. Its headlamps scour the aftermath, seeking out the remaining bales. They turn routinely over Allt Clwtpatrwm, the wood in which I had been hoping to sleep, so I climb another stile and continue north.

Cardiganshire, slowly, is leached of its colour.

Here a man on a quad is laughing hysterically.

Here, again in the Teifi Valley, I creep along the verge of the A485, while the lights of cars burst out of the corners – their speeds, for me as perhaps for deer and rabbits, such as I can barely comprehend.

5

Cockshead Wood to Coed Penbryn

15 September 2020

Sarn Helen resumes, as the B4578, a short way after Bremia Fort, home to several high-nosed llamas, which, as a subgroup including alpacas, seem these days to be Wales's third-favourite animal: the Liberal Democrats of the grazing world. The morning is muted, smeared with cloud. The low light lies on the yellow-touched poplars, and on the hills, which have stepped away so that the river, like the dismantled railway, can weave as it will across the dew-shining valley. The lane itself is perfectly straight. Its vehicles appear as gathering specks between the violet-blue harebells that hang along the verges, the purple-black sloes of the blackthorn and the bright-red berries of the guelder rose.

From the south comes a taxi full of children in uniform, the driver wearing a pale-blue face mask.

From the north come Huw Davies and Rich Morgan, Carpenters and Roofing Specialists.

Stag's Head Garage, a small, shabby place facing Hendrewen Caravan Park, sells all of the drinks and confectionery that have haunted my thoughts since leaving Llandovery. At the counter, a beaming woman of greying hair and ill-fitting jeans brews Tetley's tea, retrieves some milk, gives odds in Welsh on rain that afternoon. She turns to her till and punches in numbers – all while watching some programme on her phone and exchanging gossip with a woman in jodhpurs, whose Daihatsu Terios, idling in the forecourt, bellows out Rod Stewart's 'Sailing'. Besides the occasional face in a windscreen, these are the only people I see for some miles until a handful of larches, already half-bare, lines the way into Ty'n Celyn. Here a nuthatch is assaulting the moss of a branch. Here a first sign mentions Aberystwyth, an Openreach van offers universal fibre and drivers dither at the various junctions, peering into the still-low light. As a village, Ty'n Celyn is no bigger than its hollow: seven or eight houses of shaven lawns, dahlias and potting sheds, a dealership in 4×4s and, in the dust of an unloved bus stop, the words GWENNO A MAMGU ('Gwenno and Granny') and CYMRU RYDD ('Free Wales').

The Daihatsu passes, still playing Rod.

Put yourself west of the Cambrian Mountains, speak a bit of bad Welsh in a petrol station and it is astonishing how natural independence can seem. Everywhere along this road, in bedroom windows, on poles in gardens, you see the rearing lions of Owain Glyndŵr – the flag of an independent Wales. Back in Brecon, so far as I recall, I have not seen them once. Further east again, towards Hay-on-Wye, nationalist ambitions can seem bizarre, even absurd: the sort of thing you might expect from Moose, a local lad who, as I remember, resolved to assert his Welsh identity by cheering Germany over England during Euro '96 and had himself ejected from the Clyro pub. Perhaps it was somebody of his sort who, in 2019, sprayed COFIWCH DRYWERYN ('Remember Tryweryn') on to the road sign next to Hay Festival. First daubed (misspelt) in 1963 on a ruin near

Llanrhystud, Aberystwyth, this has become the great nationalist slogan: a cry of loss for the Gwynedd valley, home to the
Welsh-speaking village of Capel Celyn, which was flooded
in the mid-1960s to provide water for Liverpool. The original
mural has often been vandalized; these issues are complex in
every part of Wales. Still, in the months before the pandemic,
it was remarkable how, in its iconic red and white, COFIWCH
DRYWERYN appeared on over fifty other walls – and none of
them east of the Cambrian Mountains.

Given Wales's history of clearances, the attitude to these
things back in the east can seem counter-intuitive. Take the Elan
Valley Reservoirs, which send their water to Birmingham. These
were begun in 1893 and largely completed by 1896 – although
one more, Claerwen, was not opened until 1952 and public
meetings to discuss another were held as recently as the 1970s.
Among other things, they drowned a church, a chapel, a shop,
a watermill, a pair of mansions (both, briefly, home to the poet
Percy Shelley), eighteen houses and cottages and, of course, the
best of their farmland. Like the clearance of Mynydd Epynt, but
this time bolstered by 50,000 English-speaking navvies, they
spelt an end to Welsh as the local language.

'At the time,' said Robert Hughes, when we were talking at
his farm, Aberglanhirin. He was referring to the period of the
dam's construction. 'At the time there was people really ada-
mant against them, like, because Birmingham came in here and
kicked the local people out, some of them. There was no compensation or anything like that. They just came in and took it. It
was a bit rough at the time, like, but at the same time it was the
best thing that happened to Rhayader because it fetched work
in up to this very present day. It's put Rhayader on the map, like.
And the way they built them. It's a massive achievement.'

That same week, in July 2016, I went to visit May and Gwyn

Lewis, down the hill in Elan Village. May, then, was well into her seventies, retired from a life spent almost entirely on Troedrhiwdrain Farm, above Pen y Garreg Reservoir. Gwyn, her son, was in his middle fifties: a man who, as Robert put it, had been 'mad as a hatter' as a boy, but now was paralysed from the neck down, having jumped into a shallow pond for a bet when he was a teenager.

Gwyn spoke of typhoid and dysentery, of the conditions in Birmingham in the late nineteenth century.

'If I'd been living here then,' he said, 'I'd have felt differently, but it had to be done, didn't it? Like, Birmingham needed the water. All the millions of people who lived there and needed the water . . . Just a few people suffered up here. It's worth it, really, isn't it? For the many, like.'

'I tell you what,' said May, 'it was the most marvellous work of construction. It was really brilliant.'

Even those whose families had been displaced seemed to feel very much this way. Round the corner of the hill lived John Pugh, whose grandparents had been turned out of the Gro, one of the farms lost under Caban Coch Reservoir. Among John's earliest memories was sleeping next to the horse and cart that his family used to travel back from the Valleys, where they had wound up exiled for years. Now he farmed at Crawnant Fach and nurtured his own legend as a fighter – having variously, so it was said, overcome five men down in Newbridge, hurling one from the bridge into the Wye, and sanded off the nose of another on the tarmac of Newtown High Street.

'The dams,' he pronounced, in his grand, nasal voice, 'fed the factories that built the Spitfires. It was the dams put the "Great" in Great Britain.'

*

A little way east of the village of Bronant, on the grass-streaked lane here following Sarn Helen an ancient man comes shuffling along and stops at the verge where I am eating a Mars bar. He returns my greeting with a spasmic nod. His shirt is loose. There is some sort of crust in the long white stubble covering his once-pretty face.

'I'm not sitting on your lawn?' I ask, glancing round at the untamed grass between my back and a small grey house – its pebble-dash streaked by a lifetime's rain.

'Do you live here?' I ask in English, then Welsh, when the man gives no reply.

'A car just passed,' he says at last, 'and pushed me in the hedge.'

There is, in these parts of Cardiganshire, a sense of a land-scape blank, as devoid as the day's hood of cloud. There are no hills to merit the name. The mountains are a grey line scratching the horizon. There are trees, dwarfish, groping east – a female peregrine lifts from a fencepost and crosses a field with swift, easy movements, darting exactly round the contours of an oak – but there are no hedges here at all. Nor, whatever this man might say, have there been any vehicles for some time – besides the bike of a teenage girl, who must be on a circuit of the local lanes since she overtakes me, pedalling madly, every ten or fifteen minutes.

The Cambrian Mountains remain in the east. On the map Sarn Helen comes and goes, as a lane, as a dotted line; then it disappears altogether, close to a farm named Llwyn-merch-Gwilym. Blackbirds pick at the berries of a hawthorn. A marsh requires half an hour of leaping dark and greasy pools. A dingle, Cwm Groynant, descends through marshalled conifers into leaf mould, ferns and sessile oaks – and then parts for the dismantled railway.

This, I realize, would have been the railway remembered by
Cliff Pugh, another of the farmers who spoke to me in 2016.
Back then, Cliff was eighty-two years old, a compact man of
pate and tank top, living with his cousin Marlene in a bunga-
low not far from Rhayader. But for most of his life he had lived
at Bodtalog, a farm near enough at the heart of Wales, being
equidistant between north and south, between Cardigan Bay
and the English border. Two miles west of Aberglanhirin it is
an endlessness of Molinia grass, bleached and unpalatable even
to sheep. The only greens are the shelter belt of trees behind the
house and a scrap of grazing on the bank of the Elan, which is,
as it happens, the meeting point of Cardiganshire, Radnorshire
and Montgomeryshire.

The whistles of the trains would punctuate his days – just
there, on that desolate ridge – very much as, when I was a child,
we knew one o'clock by the warning siren at Dolyhir Quarry,
over Weythel Common.

Cliff was, so he explained, born in 1934 to a Welsh father and
an English mother – though his mother was, in fact, born at
Dolfaenog, one of the farms drowned by Pen y Garreg Reservoir,
and was English only in the sense that it was her first language.
It was also the language that she spoke to Cliff, who, for all of
the Cardiganshire richness of his voice, never learnt to speak
Welsh properly himself. Cliff may have been the first 'English'
farmer at Bodtalog, but in other respects, as a boy and young
man, he lived very much as six generations of his family had
lived on the farm before him. He would milk the cow and cut
the hay by hand. He would draw the water with a bucket from
the brook – 'my daughter,' he said, 'were nine year old before we
had cold running water in the house' – while washing meant a
tin bath in front of a peat fire, kindled by the ancient trees that
they would unearth on the treeless slopes.

'We never bought no coal until 1954,' he said. 'It was all peat. You can cut peat anywhere up there, and once you go down. The next depth and you'd be on silver birch, all on the wet ground, no matter where on the hill there. You'd find good trunks – felled, like that – so it must have been the bush in some generation.'

As a boy, during his seven years of school, Cliff would walk nine miles every day, to and from his lessons at Dernol Farm ('they'd have a fit, the children, if they had that now!'). In a trap pulled by a cob named Jack he would visit Rhayader, the nearest town, only twice a year: once before Christmas and once in May, for Studt's Pleasure Fair. But it was more than all and any of this. Life at Bodtalog was an entire culture of communal shearing and Sunday worship, of seasonal tramps and weeks of snow, of charmers, the traditional medical and veterinary practitioners whose work relied on principles of sympathetic magic, and stories whose antiquity can only be guessed.

'Auntie Wyn,' Cliff said, 'she always reckoned she was seeing ghosts, like. She was coming now with a pony and trap. The next thing: "I could feel someone jump up behind me on the pony, like that. I wouldn't say a word. I were riding. Then just before I get to Rhayader, he'd just off." And she was always seeing them, wasn't she, Marlene? These ghosts?'

A ghost sitting on the back of your horse is, in fact, quite a common feature of traditional local stories. About three miles from where I grew up is the forbidding, half-timbered Hergest Court. It is the former home of *The Red Book of Hergest* – one of the two sources of *The Mabinogion* – and, prior to that, to Thomas Vaughan ap Rosser, who was beheaded while fighting for the Yorkists in 1469. In death, 'Black Vaughan' proved a restless spirit. A parson is said to have challenged him, shrunk him to the size of a moth, shut him in a snuff box and dropped him in a pond, but his hauntings persisted, at least in tales. He would often, apparently, sit behind women as they rode their lonely way home from market. But it is only from Cliff that I have heard such stories attributed directly, in the way that once they must have been told.

'Was it your Auntie Blodwen or Auntie Wyn,' asked Marlene, 'who said she was coming along your road and she met hundreds of rats, and at the head was a big white rat?'

Marlene joined both my conversations with Cliff, correcting details, offering reflections. She too had lived at Bodtalog for a time – as an evacuee during the war – but otherwise she had been raised in suburban London and, improbably, had the accent and the winged glasses you might imagine of a Cockney landlady.

'That's right,' said Cliff, now chuckling merrily.

'And she said, "I knew that the rat wouldn't get out of my way. It had to be me to move out of the way of the rats, that they were led by this white rat –"'

'This white rat, at Y Gors –'

'Or the white rat would come, and she'd be smothered with rats.'

'I tell you.' Cliff shook his head. 'I don't think anybody's known such a change, in a generation, as in mine.'

It has often been observed that rural Wales saw a greater change in the thirty years after the Second World War than it had in the previous 300 years. The change was born in the war itself. Across the UK, the War Agricultural Executive Committee imposed strict quotas, payments and penalties, including the confiscation of farms, promoting a 'plough-up' campaign to put as much ground as possible to arable production, especially crops for direct human consumption. When I was a child, in fact, you could still see the wartime potato patches on the ridge of the hill across the valley. For all the horror felt by farmers at having to plough long-standing hay meadows – and, more generally, at this threat to their independence – by 1944 even the most obstreperous among them could not pretend away the results: Britain's food imports had dropped from 55 million to 12 million tons per year. Now there was the Hill Sheep Subsidy. Now there were nitrogenous fertilizers and deep digger ploughs for the bracken-covered slopes. Now, above all, there were the machines. These things, unavoidably, pointed to the future.

It could, perhaps, go unremarked that this time of change – this revolution – was entirely the result of fossil fuels, of the ability to make hydrocarbon-supported decisions. Cliff's twice-yearly visit to Rhayader ceased as soon as he had the means. A friend, a neighbour, bought a Norton 500, its tyres stuffed with hay in the absence of inner tubes, and the two of them, and often a third, would embark for whichever pub they chose, the rims of the wheels sparking on the road. Before long Cliff owned his own Royal Enfield, and not long afterwards a Ford 10 car. In 1965 he bought his first tractor, but by then the old way of life was already all but gone: its skills, its traditions, its bonds of community. Farmers now would rarely visit one another's homes and would instead travel into town. With the help of electricity, in these mountains provided by diesel generators, a whole tier of rural employment vanished: the maids, the shepherds and the labourers. And meanwhile, no longer able to compete, the smaller farms sold up to the larger, and as the landscape was drained of its people, so house after house was left to 'go down' or else to be bought by incomers – frequently as holiday homes.

The last great change in farming of these post-war decades, and equally contingent on hydrocarbons, was the development of silage, which meant that, for the first time ever, farmers could be sure that their stock would survive the winter, that their fate did not hang on the four dry days required for making decent hay. In truth, the Cambrian Mountains have never had much scope for producing winter fodder – their farmers practise a version of transhumance – but in the relative lowlands of Gladestry, back in the early 1980s, the coming of silage caused consternation. Characteristically enough, it was my father, a keen-eyed reader of *Farmers Weekly*, who persuaded a company in Brecon to produce a roll of enormous plastic bags and, with our 1954 Fordson Major and a New Holland baler built for straw but able to compress grass into things like giant eggs, brought in the valley's first silage crop. This provoked delight throughout the village. Nineteen eighty-one proved a perfect year for hay – the old ways, it seemed, had prevailed – and, for all of the camaraderie among the neighbours, there was no pleasure greater than an innovation failed. The trouble was that, the next year, the summer was a washout. The hay in the fields was reduced to slime. It was a disaster for everyone – except, that is, for us.

'How I hated watching those hay crops disappear,' my father told me recently. 'It had been going on for centuries but it made it no easier.'

By 1983, with a Ford 3000 once belonging to my grandfather, my father and a couple of other men were making silage on contract everywhere: a success for the process, as he would put it, as inevitable as it was catastrophic. Where hay-making needs to wait, normally until July when the bulk of the sap has left the grass, silage can be harvested long before – before the plants have come into flower, before the chicks of such ground-nesting birds as curlew, lapwing and yellow wagtail have had a chance to fledge. And, since there is no cause to wait, many farmers will simply hurry it all along and cover their fields in fertilizer.

There has been no aspect of this revolution without its dark corollary.

'All those wild flowers coming up,' said Cliff, 'they've lost them all now. I wish I'd had a camera then to take photographs of them. Those ones with, like, four leaves, and that yellow one, I don't know what they're called. And the hardheads, as we used to call them ...'

'There'd be yellowhammers, peewits, curlews ...' said May Lewis. 'There'd be birds, then, from bottom to top!'

'I've seen curlews up here, like,' said Robert Hughes. 'I haven't seen a bugger lately, I'm sure I haven't. I haven't heard their sound for bloody years.'

'From the age of five,' said John Pugh, 'I would walk to Llanwrthwl School, and I can remember the council men working on the road, and I could not hear them for the morning chorus!'

'What we need,' said Gerwyn Davies of Penyworlod Farm, Crickadarn, 'is people living back in the country, because even though you think the mechanization of farming is efficient, there is so much to be said for hands-on, labour-intensive work on a small patch of land. We need a more agrarian society. We need our priorities in life to change. Originally, my grandad would have chosen what was best according to what he knew about his land. Every crop you can imagine would have been on that farm. He had all the different feeds for the animals – oats, barley. There'd be wheat. They'd bake their own bread. He'd sell veg in Builth. Most of the fields were split in four, and each of them had its own name. That's how specific farming was then. Now ... It's like, if you choose any bit of land and say, "We're going to farm it this way, whatever," then you're going to need chemical and mechanical help, and both of those will have a detriment. And, as you make the situation worse, the only thing you can do to make the land productive will make it worse again. You'll get poorer and poorer ground, and less and less wildlife ...'

Gerwyn and I were talking in 2019 – as it happens, on my son's tenth birthday. It was shortly after four in the morning and, as part of an XR action, we were locked together in central London, not far from the Home Office, having just endured seven hours of police officers shouting abuse, kicking us and holding high-powered torches to our eyes until we could not tell the light from the pain.

It was our third night of almost no sleep.

It was so cold that Gerwyn seemed to be convulsing.

'Well, it just can't last,' I said.

'Well, that's it. It's like wringing that last bit of water out of a flannel. We're just wringing it, trying to squeeze out the last few drops, thinking that we can keep wringing it, and you just can't.'

It was only in 1959 that archaeologists realized that Trawsgoed has a Roman fort. It is difficult to know why it took them so long. There are indications wherever you look. The River Ystwyth, here, is not the bleak little stream whose source lies just to the west of Bodtalog, nor is it the poisonous torrent which passes among the Cwmystwyth lead mines, their lifeless screes and humps of spoil – without water birds, without fish. Even in this hat-collapsing drizzle, the Ystwyth is plainly a river of which the Romans would have approved, like the Teifi at Llanio, like the Tywi at Llandovery. It is overhung by lush sweet chestnuts, beeches and oaks almost on the scale of those which stand in the broad, flat fields, between the fat, grazing cattle and the thickly wooded hills. Visit Pumsaint, visit Y Gaer, and you will need no map to know that there was a fort on this rising ground, behind this ivy-covered wall and this tumult of laurels, which gird, seal off Crosswood Park.

'That's Ivor's land,' says a woman at a nearby stables. Her grimace apparently explains itself. 'There's not much there to be honest with you. You wouldn't be missing a lot ...'

If nothing else, you can say for sure that the Romans and the Vaughans, the family who established Crosswood Park in the seventeenth century, could recognize some quality farmland. Following this avenue of immense limes, passing a sign to the Mansion House, the Orangery, the Estate Office and the Garden Lodge, you pass a John Deere 6230R spreading manure in a red-brown field pushing all of forty acres. By the time you can see the house itself – a Georgian pile with a Victorian wing, like some moribund prep school, the bursar, maybe, having absconded with the fees and the matron – you are surrounded by the lawns of Ffarmers at scale: a vision of intensified production, fertilized to luminescence. There is not so much as a flower to be seen. There is not even a hedge between yourself and the first low slope, where the weatherboard gables of five enormous cattle sheds stand alongside silos like Soviet rockets, silage clamps, slurry pits and ranks of tractors whose value, surely, must run into the millions of pounds. No Zetor 6245 reveals itself. No tatty dog yelps on his length of chain. As for any sign of a farmer, as I wander the concrete, peering through doors at mysterious machines, I encounter only one young man who looks up from his phone to return my smile as he paces along in his black-leather shoes.

According to the sign beside the lane, Trawsgoed Farm is managed by IBERS, Judith Thornton's department at Aberystwyth University.

'Bioscience for the future,' it says.

*

The Paith, a swampy and alder-choked stream, marks the edge of the territory thought once to have belonged to St Padarn. It issues from the hill north of Llanfihangel-y-Creuddyn, running west towards a seeming cloud, which resolves into the evening-gleaming sea. According to his thirteenth-century *Life*, which conflates him with two quite different bishops, Padarn was born in the early sixth century into a noble Breton family, trained under Illtyd at Llantwit Major and became abbot of his own monastery, Llanbadarn Fawr, just inland of Aberystwyth. As the story goes, the ground between the Paith and the River Rheidol was granted to the saint by the local governor – partly by way of compensation for his followers' beheading of Reaus, Padarn's servant, partly out of awe and fear when Padarn simply replaced the head and restored Reaus to life.

There are reasons other than colour and incident to return to the *Lives* of the saints. However distorted, they do preserve some history, some genuine insight into former times. The *Life* of St Padarn might be largely improbable, but it does, for example, remember Llanbadarn Fawr as an episcopal see separate to the see of St David's and therefore contains at least one element dating from the Age of Saints – or, at any rate, from before AD 720. The *Life* also has a fascination with heads, which is, it seems, more ancient again and is common to many of the stories of the saints. Take Justinian, a particularly ascetic hermit who is said to have been beheaded on Ramsay Island and, after a spring burst from the ground, to have collected his head and walked across the sound to be buried at the chapel which still bears his name. Or Decuman, who went better again. When his head was severed by a Somerset pagan, he set it directly back on his neck and then walked home across the Bristol Channel to Rhoscrowther in Pembrokeshire.

Many of these stories contain the same elements. In the *Life* of St Beuno, the rapacious King Caradog pursues the beautiful, virginal Gwenffrewi, catches her at the door of a church and slices off her head with a sword. Her body stays outside, her head rolls inside and where her blood falls there issues a spring. (Beuno, witnessing this event, curses Caradog, who melts into a lake, then replaces the head and revives the girl.) Which has echoes of the story of Eluned, one of Brychan's numerous children, a virgin beheaded on Slwch Tump near Brecon, whose head goes rolling away down the slope – a spring erupting where at last it stops. Which has echoes of the story of Dunad, the 'most happy virgin' in *The Life of St David*, who is invited by her stepmother, the wife of Bwya, the infamous Irish 'chieftain and druid', to come and gather nuts in the woods of Glyn Hodnant. There the stepmother has the girl lie on her lap so as to arrange her hair. This done, she cuts off her head and a fountain good for various ailments rises where the blood meets the earth.

Of course, Celtic Christianity did not have a monopoly when it came to beheadings, but still it is worth reflecting on Padarn and Reaus in light of a story like that last. Here is a girl, a virgin, who has her hair ceremoniously dressed and is then beheaded in a hazel wood, her blood giving rise to a healing spring. Though written in the eleventh century, it is a tale, plainly, containing relics of a very early tradition – given the druidical associations with hazel trees and sacrifice, and that Bwya himself is explicitly called a druid, and that springs, like lakes, possess a well-attested ancient significance, sometimes as the home of a deity, sometimes, as in the legend of Llyn y Fan Fach, as a boundary between this world and Annwfn, the Celtic Otherworld.

The head seems to have played a central role throughout pre-Christian Celtic culture. Evidence for a Celtic head cult can be found in Classical accounts: Diodorus Siculus describes how, after battle, Celts would embalm with cedar oil the heads of their more eminent enemies and hang those of others from the necks of their horses. You find it too in such archaeological sites as the sanctuary in Roquepertuse, Provence, where the portico has cavities to receive human skulls. Nor does Welsh legend want for such traditions. There could hardly be a better illustration of the power thought to reside in the head than the 'Second Branch of the Mabinogi'. In this tale, Bendigeidfran, the giant King of Britain, leads his fleet to Ireland to avenge offence done to his sister, Branwen. He himself wades between the kingdoms since no ship is able to hold him. On arrival, a wary peace gives way to slaughter on a majestic scale: five pregnant women alone survive to repopulate the whole of Ireland, while, other than Branwen, only seven remain of the entire British force. Bendigeidfran, fatally poisoned, instructs his men to cut off his head and carry it to London. His men then spend eighty-seven years on feasting, first in Harlech then on the island of Gwales, off Pembrokeshire. But in the end they do as bade and bury the king's head on White Hill – possibly the site of the Tower of London – with his face turned towards France, to preserve Britain from foreign invasion.

6

Coed Penbryn to Machynlleth

16 September 2020

The dew is heavy during the night; there are times when you might take it for rain. In Coed Penbryn, above the Melindwr Valley, the water ticks and pops on the leaves, with fuller pops on the dead leaves around me and on my bivvy bag. Occasionally an acorn lands with a thwack. Between my long, deep washes of sleep, a tawny owl gives his hollow cry; some small creature scrabbles through the bracken; the sky, by increments, reveals itself: a silver river through the black of the trees. Sessile oaks are precision itself. An ash will sprawl, sit an elbow on the ground. A beech, for all its dignity, will permit its branches to collide or even to bury themselves in the trunk. A sessile oak, all mossy and gaunt and bound to some hard, rocky slope, will never indulge such sloppiness. Its measurement, its appreciation of space will keep every dense, lobed leaf apart, every twig a discreet distance from the next – that distance more discreet again if the twig belongs to a different tree.

Somewhere in the valley a crow is annoyed.

Somewhere on the hill the sheep are growing restive; their calls gather in number and volume with the calls of a farmer, the sputter of his quad.

Achingly, I restore my clothes, force my feet back into their boots and then fumble in the neck of my rucksack. I have dug out my book, my anorak, my plastic trousers and three pairs of socks before I remember that my food is finished – that I no longer have so much as a biscuit. On every side, among the bracken and the bilberries, the grass is knit with silver-white cobwebs: hammocks as much as a foot across, each strand strung with microscopic droplets, shining together in the growing light. The sky between the leaves has turned a faint, pale blue. As the farmer's quad retreats across the hillside, so the calls of the sheep subside, fade back into a car on a lane, a lorry on the A44, the background thunder of an aeroplane: the perpetual noise of vehicles, which masquerades as quiet.

In Goginan, the A44 sends its morning traffic east towards the Cambrian Mountains, west towards Aberystwyth and the coast. There is a pub, the Druid Inn, and a dog-grooming service named Posh Paws. There is a line of pressed-together houses, peering north into a body of mist, but no sign of the post office claimed by Google – though I check every window of its supposed building, a former schoolhouse with a Reliant Robin rusting in its yard. Along the pavement, his collie on a string, comes a man direct from a Niall Griffiths novel: a rangy figure, smoking fiercely, tattoos bleeding from his loose grey hoodie on to his hands and his close-cropped head.

I greet him, ask about a nearby shop.

'You'd be lucky,' he says, in an almost-trill. 'It's either Ponterwyd, and you don't want to be walking up that road, or else it's got to be down in Aber.' He pauses, pulls a reflective face. 'There did used to be one in Capel Bangor. Nice walk too. Couple of miles and plenty of sheep. You can get sick of the sheep, mind, can't you?'

These last words he addresses to his dog.

Though Sarn Helen, once, must have led north from Trawsgoed to the forts at Erglodd and Pennal, it has left no trace on the OS map. The reason would seem to be reasonably obvious. The Romans' devotion to the shortest route can only have faltered in the face of these slopes – each of them that bit more grand, that bit more like those of North Wales, with their tumbling woods and their craggy crests and their sheep in apparent rebuttal of gravity. It is a problem that, somehow, can go overlooked when it comes to talking about Wales and its infrastructure. For instance, you will often hear it lamented that if you wish to travel by train between the north and south of the country, then you will have to spend most of your journey in England – as if this amounts to a seizure of autonomy, not a simple result of the fact that the Marches are relatively flat. In Wales, the M4, the North Wales Expressway, the North Wales Coast Line and the South Wales Main Line – in fact, most of the principal transport links – all keep within a few miles of the sea, while the A470, the current north–south artery, is an awkward, snaking sort of a road, usually clogged by a camper van or a lorry trailing bits of straw. Wales, in the end, is a lot of wet hills: hills which rarely align with your purpose and, whatever their history of extraction, result in a landscape – and a culture – comprising a collection of drainage basins.

The Elan Valley speaks only English.

The neighbouring Ystwyth Valley speaks Welsh too.

Perhaps, then, the Romans simply followed these lanes and even climbed this mist-swallowed path: this opaque ring of well-grazed grass, occasionally including a few swampy trees or one or two small, rich-coated sheep, which fade as they turn and then disappear. The hill goes on. The hill goes on. Despite the moist, autumnal air the sweat falls steadily from my chin. And, as if the slope is not enough, a farmer seems to have devoted his lockdown to making the way as impassable as possible. Now there is a fence where there ought to be a kissing gate. Now there is a post hole where there ought to be a sign. At one point a narrow bridge has been sealed completely with barbed wire. There is, in fact, every imaginable obstacle save that used by our neighbour, years ago, who believed that the vet was training pheasants to attack him and would wire an electric fence to every gate on the paths of his farm.

In the long queue for the counter of the Nisa Local in the BP Garage in Penrhyncoch, you can only be struck by how white we all are. Here is a white and upright lady, her dyed-brown hair cut into a bowl, the *Cambrian News* furled under one arm as she pays for her petrol with a last '*Diolch*' – 'Thanks' – and heads for the door and her green Toyota Starlet. Here is a white man with grizzled moustache, a builder to judge by the logo on his T-shirt, peeling the cellophane from his Benson & Hedges before the boy at the till has even swiped his coffee. All the way along Sarn Helen, in fact, two things have been absolutely consistent: there has not been a second of the day or night without the noise of an aeroplane, and there has not been a single person of colour. Of course, the route is almost all rural; you can hardly miss the rural-urban ethnic divide anywhere across the UK. All the same, the language must play its part. I have attended Welsh course on Welsh course, on which initially there would be twelve or fifteen students, almost all of them incomers – then would come the mutating letters and the words without the faintest relationship to anything outside of Breton or Cornish, and, for all of their constituent music, within weeks there would be two of us left. Come from a non-white ethnic background, and you might think a move to Anglophone Wales already challenge enough.

Through the window, next to a selection of greeting cards, the mist truncates the hills around Aberystwyth.

I shove my basket of sandwiches, pasties, Lucozade and McVitie's flapjacks forward by another foot.

The fact of the language contains at once all that is best and worst in Wales. If you visit Ireland and mention your provenance, you can hardly escape the question: how, *how* can Welsh be so robust? How, according to the latest census, are 29 per cent of the population able now to speak the language – an increase of 4 per cent in just ten years?

And the answer is: it is that important. We – Wales – stand together in the Principality Stadium and bellow in conclusion to the national anthem, '*O bydded i'r hen iaith barhau*' ('O may the old language endure') and you will not experience a moment more fervent. The Welsh language is the lifeblood of an independent people, of a culture's endurance against all the odds. This is, after all, the only part of the Western Roman Empire that managed to resist the Barbarian hordes.

And the answer is: it is too important. Wales has never played the Celtic trick of spreading its identity over multiple bases, or not to any great effect. No lone piper in Royal Stewart Tartan stands astride a Gwynedd peak. No ranks of girls in leprechaun green go step-dancing down the Rhondda Valley. In Wales, the language carries it all – and this does, of course, reflect an inward-looking trait. Historians will sometimes point to rules of inheritance in medieval Welsh law. For centuries, the principle of *cyfran* – of dividing property equally between male heirs – was essential to the country's culture. Primogeniture – conferring property only on the first-born son – was imposed on Wales in 1543, with the Second Act of Union, but in practice it has never really prevailed. The basic scenario applies as ever. Forced to seek out an estate of their own, the younger sons of the Norman lords mass hungrily along the Welsh border, while the Welsh squabble over the same soggy field. They look inwards, ever inwards – and if this is your culture, so that argument suggests, then where is the need to speak a language that anyone else understands?

And the answer is: it is national policy. For centuries, the English language was promoted in Wales and the Welsh language was repressed. The Blue Books – the 1847 parliamentary report which denounced the Welsh as backward and immoral, placing much of the blame on their language – left scars which remain to this day. It is among the ambitions of the Welsh government that, by 2050, there will be a million people in Wales able to speak Welsh as well as English, and the merits of their case are obvious. For all its remarkable recent success, the future of the language remains uncertain. Naturally, though, in a country so fragmented, this principle of promoting Welsh means different things in different places – depending, as it does, on a definition of Welshness more resonant here in Ceredigion, where 60.1 per cent of the population are to some extent bilingual, than in Gladestry, where I grew up, where locally only English has been spoken for the better part of 300 years. The village sign illustrates the situation. At the bottom is the 'English' name, Gladestry – probably, in fact, a corrupted Welsh name, comprising a personal name plus *tre*, or 'homestead' – while at the top, occupying two full lines, is the 'Welsh' name, Llanfair Llythynwg: a corrupted version of Llanfair Llwyth Yfynwg, meaning 'St Mary's Church in the Lands of Yfynwg', whose last previous recorded use was in 1566 and which, locally at least, is not used by anyone at all.

That sign encapsulates the tensions of the borders, and to that extent the tensions of my life. Like many other writers I know, I would, until recently, have been called 'Anglo-Welsh'. The official term now is 'Welsh writer in English' – although to be simply a 'Welsh writer' is still to be a writer in the Welsh language. I think of a writer friend from Brecon who has never felt 'allowed to identify as Welsh'. And another, from Swansea, whose instinct when asked about her writing in English is a sorrow, yes, at not knowing her 'own language' but, beneath that, a consuming shame. My own response to this hierarchy was, for many years, equally deferential. I would always, had I had the choice, have voted for Llanfair Llythynwg as the first name on the sign. But then came the 2008 Wales Book of the Year award – its English-language shortlist including *The Claude Glass*, my first Radnorshire novel. The ceremony was held in the ballroom of the Hilton Cardiff Hotel, and I can honestly say that I had never in my life wished for anything so fiercely as I wished to win that day – for the validation, the acceptance. And, true, for the £10,000. The speeches complete, Rhodri Glyn Thomas, then the Heritage Minister, read out the winner and read out my name. I walked between the tables to the steps of the stage, congratulations on every side, when it became apparent that something was wrong. Somebody came hurrying to whisper to the minister. After that, my memories are few. I remember walking out of the ballroom, but as if seeing myself from the outside: new-cut hair, a high-neck jacket. I can picture the hotel toilets. I vaguely remember sitting with Charlie, parked in the lay-by in Libanus. I remember better the succeeding days, when she and I tried to vanish in Pembrokeshire, as the footage of the

minister correcting himself and giving the award instead to
Dannie Abse spread across the country and across the world –
when it reached Australia my website crashed, when it reached
the US my website crashed – as my inbox and answerphone
overflowed with messages of sympathy and offers to emote on
breakfast television.

For some years the footage was a stalwart of 'blooper' programmes; I could tell when it had been recently shown by the
looks I would get in town.

I still couldn't tell you what went wrong.

As with any horrible incident, it took me a while to see clearly
again – eventually, to understand that my whole approach to
Wales would have to be rebuilt. My deference to the Welsh cultural establishment had been blown apart. My next Radnorshire
novel, *Addlands*, which did not come for another eight years, is
an emphatically local story, dispensing with the wider notions
of nation that preoccupy many of the characters in *The Claude
Glass*. In *Addlands* there is no mention of the border, nor of
England, nor of Wales. Its characters, like Cliff Pugh or May
Lewis, the real people of the mid-Wales hills, do not look elsewhere for a sense of identity; they are as ambivalent to pressures
from the west as they are to pressures from the east. These days,
that is, I would vote for Gladestry as the first name on the sign.
Not out of any disrespect for the Welsh language. Just because, if
you are to write truthfully, then you must allow in the tensions.
You cannot defer to a political agenda, however admirable that
agenda may be, if the price is not to acknowledge the things that
are actually there.

If anywhere is the home of Welsh-language culture, then perhaps it is Talybont. The village lies deep among pine woods and

rolling, swelling, gorse-pocked grass. It holds up its head with surprising effect, given the quantity of motorbikes, camper vans and Range Rovers with personalized number plates fighting both ways along the road at its heart. Next to the road is a triangle of grass with a couple of benches and, lining the pavement, fruit of lockdown, scores of brightly painted stones originally, surely, from the beach at Borth. The sky has cleared to a brilliant blue. Rest for a minute on one of the benches and you are seized by the sense of vitality in the place – in the houses all on different levels, deep-blue, turquoise, white and gold above their tiny, stone-walled gardens; in the villas set back into the pigeon-flapping slopes with their big bay windows and red-brick chimneys, each with its analogue television aerial. In palette and in atmosphere, all of these serve to frame the village's centrepiece: a mural, facing the northbound traffic. This gable wall belongs to Y Lolfa, the first of the publishing houses born of the revival of the Welsh language in the 1960s and 1970s. Here, three storeys high, are Gwynfor Evans, the first Plaid Cymru MP, beaming and raising a hand to the traffic; Eirwyn Pontshân, the entertainer, holding high the bottle of Welsh milk that he deemed better than English beer; and Nan Bowyer, the iconic protestor, with her long blonde hair and her long black coat and her placard reading '*Carchar am garu'i iaith!*' ('Prison for loving the language!').

And on a hill just to the north – or so a sign would have you believe – lies the most iconic of all the Welsh-language writers: Taliesin himself.

Taliesin makes his historical appearance in *Historia Brittonum*, a manuscript of the early ninth century traditionally attributed to Nennius, which describes him as one of the five great poets of Britain in the late sixth century. From the earliest 'Taliesin' poems, too, he seems to have been a bard in the courts of the Old North: the post-Roman British kingdoms of Northern England and Southern Scotland, which had, by about 700, mostly fallen to the Picts and the Germanic tribes. Taliesin, however, is not just Taliesin. That is, the poetry that bears his name, as collected in the *Book of Taliesin*, ranges in date from perhaps the sixth to the thirteenth centuries, and ranges in subject from the praise of kings to medieval 'prophetic' material. The name Taliesin, it seems, became a 'persona', a channel for a voice of myth, the model of a bard in the ecstasy of inspiration, straddling both ancient lore and contemporary Christian learning.

More, Taliesin is a figure of legend. He appears as a courtier to Arthur in 'How Culhwch Won Olwen' and a follower of Bendigeidfran in the 'Second Branch of the Mabinogi' – indeed, he is named as one of the seven British men to survive that war in Ireland. He is a sage, a sorcerer, a druid, even a shaman, able to exist outside his given form:

> I was path, I was eagle,
> I was a coracle at sea.
> I was bubbles in beer,
> I was a raindrop in a shower ...

According to *Hanes Taliesin*, a manuscript compiled in the sixteenth century, Taliesin was originally Gwion Bach, a servant of the lake-dwelling goddess Ceridwen charged with stirring a cauldron containing a potion of poetic inspiration. This was intended for Ceridwen's son, but three drops landed on Gwion's hand, which he then put into his mouth, taking the magic upon himself. He fled, pursued by his furious mistress, both metamorphosing as they went – he into a hare and she into a greyhound, he into a salmon and she into an otter, he into a bird and she into a hawk, he into a grain of wheat and she into a hen, which promptly ate it up. The seed, though, impregnated Ceridwen and Gwion Bach was born again, so beautiful that she could not bring herself to kill him and instead abandoned him to the sea. It was somewhere not far from here, between Aberystwyth and the Dyfi Estuary, that he was saved by Elffin, son of Gwyddno Garanhir, king of the land of Cantre'r Gwaelod.

It was Elffin who named him Taliesin, meaning 'Shining Brow'.

But then the poem 'The Great Song of the World' has him created of the seven elements: earth, fire, water, air, flowers, mist and southerly wind.

All of these things must graze your mind as you stand at Bedd Taliesin – not because of the grave itself, which is a miserable affair on a shabby verge, like a dolmen erected by Spinal Tap, but because of its position, because of its outlook. It is a place worthy of a *llan*, a church. There, past the sheds of the neighbouring farm, the narrow fields and just-glimpsed woods shelve towards the Roman fortlet at Erglodd. There, past Cors Fochno, a rare 'raised' bog, are the grass-feathered dunes of Ynyslas where, as teenagers, we would come to consume magic mushrooms, and the groyne-divided sands where, with some low tides, you can see the stumps of the ancient forest which must have fed the legend of Cantre'r Gwaelod – that is, the flooding of the land by Cardigan Bay. There, above a rough stone wall where a few sheep are hiding in a sliver of shadow, the River Dyfi weaves among its golden sandbanks, between low, marshy fields and the long, pale beach that stretches west from Aberdyfi. That grey-blue band is as clear a division between north and south as there is to be found in Wales – even now, in this two o'clock haze, which renders ghostly the mountains of Gwynedd, which confounds the sea and sky. This whole scene might embody Taliesin's vision of

the three realms of medieval art: humanity, God and the living
world – all of them a unity, ecstatically alive:

> Sweet are the berries at harvest time;
> Sweet, also, is wheat on the stem ...

> Sweet are fruit blossoms high in a tree;
> Sweet, too, is to reconcile with the Creator ...

> Sweet are the fish in the shining lake;
> Sweet, too, is water's play of light and dark.

Consider this man in the field beneath* ... Two miles north of
Bedd Taliesin, close to a farm named Cefngweiriog, a man in
a Land Rover is creeping down a bank, following a couple of
dozen sheep, a collie flying to either side. He whistles and curses,
for the most part in English. He drags on the handbrake and
spills from the door, his overalls filthy, his cap tipped back, a
stick in his hand like a spear to be hurled:

'Damme, dog, I swear to God!'

His words fall into an incoherent scream.

His shoulders collapse as the first of the ewes bolts for the
space that the dogs have left.

It brings back an occasion on Hergest Ridge, gathering sheep
on the common land when I was eight or nine years old. Three
of our ewes had strayed across the deep valley on to the head
of Hanter Hill. Finally my father, having tried every curse and
received little more than a reproachful look, seized our dog,
Jim, by the scruff and flung him after them, away down the

---

* 'Affinity', R.S. Thomas

slope. It brings back a story he told me once of attending a hedging course, of standing in a gaggle of other young men – on Disgwylfa Hill, as I remember – while, on the naked hillside opposite, a farmer slowly sank to his knees, lifted his face to an empty sky and implored: 'Why me? Why me?'

The track goes on, not obstinately straight and certainly not marked on the map as Roman – although, when the landscape allows, it does appear to point at Cefn Caer, the fort at Pennal on the north bank of the Dyfi, a couple of miles west of Machynlleth. It crosses an ivy-hanging, fern-dripping gorge. It turns along a miniature, oak-cloaked valley without so much as a stream to its name. It skirts a marsh left by the last glaciation, and a bonsai mountain like you see in North Wales. Here the ash trees are rusty with numberless keys, the rowan trees are scarcely more than their berries and the crab apple trees are scarcely more than their fruit – the autumn, just these few miles north, being that much more advanced even than it was in Ffarmers.

The birches and larches are both a thick bronze.

The beeches have left drifts of leaves thin and vivid against each verge.

The farmers who are actually here in Wales, working these wet, knotted hills, are rarely if ever to be found in books – even in the poetry of R. S. Thomas. The characters of Thomas's first period – the period between 1946 and 1968, inspired by his years in Manafon, Montgomeryshire – are often to be found at work in the fields, but these are not men like other men, with an inner life and a place in society. Although always subject to 'your curious gaze', they experience no obvious sense of exposure. It is not a part of Thomas's picture that, should one get a tractor stuck, or break ranks and hazard a silage crop, they will do so in full view of their community. His farmers, who coalesce in his best-known character, Iago Prytherch, are 'frightening in the[ir] vacancy'. They exist without feeling or reflection. More than once Thomas insists on their humanity – 'Listen, listen, I am a man like you' – and yet, in insisting, he seems to cast doubt. Prytherch he even calls 'your prototype' – as though he stands in relation to you, the reader, and to the people of Wales in general, like an ape or a Neanderthal.

> Iago Prytherch his name, though, be it allowed,
> Just an ordinary man of the bald Welsh hills,
> Who pens a few sheep in a gap of cloud.
> Docking mangels, chipping the green skin
> From the yellow bones with a half-witted grin
> Of satisfaction . . .

Look for the prototype in literature of Iago Prytherch and you can do worse than the leech-gatherer: the man described by William Wordsworth in his 1802 lyric poem 'Resolution and Independence'. The two creations have much in common. Both are ancient beyond measure – the leech-gatherer seems the 'oldest man . . . that ever wore grey hairs', while Thomas's labourer 'has been here since life began' – and both, in their imagery as in their lives, are shown to be in a state of nature. Prytherch 'Endur[es] like a tree'. At first sight the leech-gatherer seems 'a huge stone' – even if his voice, when he speaks, 'to me was like a stream'. Both are alone among the lakes and the woods, remote from their fellows and even their creators, who make no attempt to inhabit them as characters. And as such, either one might serve as a model for the people commonly depicted in the writing of rural Wales.

Open perhaps the best-known example, Bruce Chatwin's 1982 novel *On the Black Hill*, and you will learn that Lewis

Jones 'always wore a puzzled look', that Benjamin Jones would use his nose 'in conversation as a weapon' and that both 'had the reputation of being incredibly stingy', but you will not learn these things from the twins themselves. Theirs is a story 'told', not 'shown'; we are never invited to participate directly in the experiences of the characters. Here, again, are men of nature, half-lost to the rain, to the jays, to the hazels. Here, again, are men of the margins – their house, the Vision, is literally divided by the Wales–England border – but margins which have been essentially confected for the purposes of drama. At one point, at the local railway station, Benjamin shrieks 'Dirty Saxon!' at a belligerent porter who has himself been abusing a drunk as 'Taffy': an exchange of a sort, I will stake my soul, which has never taken place anywhere along the Radnorshire–Herefordshire border.

If you come from the 88 per cent of Wales given over to agriculture and turn to your representation in literature, you may find that you experience a very minor version of the 'double consciousness' described by W. E. B. Du Bois: a sense of seeing yourself through other people's eyes. The person you are shown is consistently primitive, a peasant remote from the modern world and so requiring explanation, a custodian of ancient lore more at ease among the birds and the trees: a person who always inhabits the edges, never the centre, of a fictional world.

7

Machynlleth to Cedris Farm

19 October 2020

Newtown mingles with the lights, the reflections, the people in their face masks spaced along the bus: a man in a brown-leather jacket, his white hair trailing into a mullet; two elderly women with the usual perms but with harder vowels than the vowels at home. It feels, as it often does, forgotten in the wastes of its green-grey hills. It feels bent beneath the prospect of the new national lockdown, due in only four days' time, of a winter reduced to ourselves in our rooms. We turn on to New Road, pass a derelict glazier's, pass terraced houses whose small bay windows shimmer with breakfast television. To the right, St David's Church stands on its incline, all buttresses and spirelets. Grand as it appears, for fifteen years it has been empty even of its rood screen, which has tantalizing traces of its original Tudor paintwork and can now be found on the gallery of St Llwchaiarn's Church, Llanllwchaiarn.

It feels, on this colourless autumn morning, impossible to believe that this town was once home to the Newtown

Workshop, source of the most astonishing ecclesiastical wood-
work anywhere to be found in Wales – or, across the border, in
Cheshire and Herefordshire. Take Llananno Church, which we
passed at dawn, a few miles north of Llandrindod Wells. If you
pause on your way up the A483 and enter that drab Victorian
building which you could easily ignore every day of your life,
you will find yourself facing a brow of oak: a late-medieval
screen and loft of such conviction, such finesse that you can
only halt inside the door, held by its presence, its physical
heft. Then, perhaps, you will notice Christ, the apostles and
prophets who occupy the twenty-five canopied niches, or the
tracery heads at the top of each bay: the lacework, almost, of
Catherine wheels and other geometric forms, which hangs from
its underside, precise in the light of the chancel window. But
these are only a taste of its riches. There are the panels which
curve above your head, continuing, elaborating these designs –
divided by bosses of intricate knotwork, flowers, a man's face
with pendulous jowls. There are the horizontal trails. One is
a vine, each end spewing from the jaws of a wyvern. Another
is a pomegranate, symbol of Aragon and, since the work was
completed around 1500, of Catherine of Aragon's marriage to
Prince Arthur, the ill-fated brother of Henry VIII – of the hope
in Wales then invested in the (Welsh by origin) Tudor dynasty.
And then there is the boss above the door, on the chancel side,
depicting a pair of faces merged – it has three eyes, two noses,
two solemn mouths – which is most likely the Roman god
Janus.

Such is the cultural confidence that Wales has known.

Now the traffic lights change and the bus swings left, past
the near-empty car parks of Ladywell Shopping Centre and the
offices of Ladywell House. Market Street reveals itself, its charity
shops apparently abandoned. It is replaced by Charlies Stores,

which, in happier times, sells clothes and shoes, cookware and soft furnishings.

Jutting from its end wall, above a green wheelie bin, a sign reads 'CAUTION PROTRUDING SIGN'.

All of a sudden, Newtown is marvellous.

My friend Jay Griffiths is waiting in Machynlleth: a small, trim woman in walking boots, her rucksack like some monstrous hunch, rearing a full head above her own. Jay is a fascinating person to observe. Call up a photograph and you will see: gold-brown hair with a touch of disorder; gold-brown eyes, a level gaze; nostrils particularly to appreciate, being delicate, with the slightest arch, as if she possesses a superior sense of smell. But the photographs miss the main event, which is her perpetual occupation. Not a busyness, not exactly – more a total awareness, an attending-to-all-things, which has a way of gathering you up, so that you can walk clean out of Machynlleth, cross the bridge into Gwynedd, weave for half a mile along the A493, scale a gate and come on to a footpath and only then really notice that you have set out.

The fields beside the river are quiet and level, their sheep collected in wary groups, their hawthorns and hazels, long ago hedges, reduced to their bones and a few tatty leaves of purple, ochre, russet, gold. The hill to the north is rusting oaks. From the far bank two black, white-blazed horses watch as we negotiate a bog, as we admire an oak on an outcrop of shale, an effusion of the rock as it appears, as we climb through a flood-line of sticks and plastic towards a large stone house on a prominence and, a few yards beyond, several tin-roofed sheds with another in the early stages of erection.

The farmer, a man of thick sandy hair and eyes in a

weather-cut body of lines, takes a couple of moments to guide us through its mire of excavator tracks.

He levels a boot at the nearest flotsam.

His farm, he says, in answer to my question, flooded twice back in July. On one of those occasions, he received two calls in the night: alerts from Natural Resources Wales warning that water was on its way. Not that he was asleep anyway, what with worrying about all the rain. With the mountains and the narrowness of the valley upstream, the river tends to rise very quickly. Not that he was remotely surprised. It's just, he says, the way it's going these days: flooded winters, hot, dry springs, July and August flooded again.

He looks at the sky, gives a click of his tongue. The Precipice Walk, he suggests. When we get to Dolgellau, we should allow time for the Precipice Walk.

Another mile west, approaching Pennal, another bank gazes over long, marshy flats, gleaming pools and rows of gaunt willows: the River Dyfi at its navigable limit; the mountains tumbling from the north and south, converging on the river's mouth. Though the morning is motionless, warm and pearly, you can see the effects of the westerly winds all over Cefn Caer Auxiliary Fort in its half-bald hedges and its windbreak trees, even perhaps in the cab of the quad bike which drops over contours that must have been ramparts, rounding up sheep at the lick of a collie. Centuries and the deep digger plough have erased all other trace of the Romans. Back in the 1580s, William Camden could report that 'From the fort to the waterside is a broad hard way of pitched pebbles and other stones, continued in a strait line through meadows and marsh-grounds' – the waterside having provided a quay, both for a ferry and for sea-going ships. These contours are all that remain to give some sense of the course of Sarn Helen between Erglodd and the Eden

Valley, some way to the north of Dolgellau – though, of course, there is a wealth of local historians, of soldiers still using their ranks, retired vicars and headmasters, who always have views on this sort of subject. Most suggest that the road ran east of Cadair Idris, following the Dulas and the Llefenni Valleys, but some contend that it ran west around the coast, via Aberdyfi, Tywyn and Fairbourne, while others again point to the OS maps – 1921 and 1947 editions – which show a Roman road running due north of Pennal, directly over the ridge of the mountain.

'For many societies,' says Jay, 'the most extreme form of punishment has been isolation from the group, from the tribe – because nobody can survive alone and because it's not just a physical punishment, it's emotional, it's psychological ... In most cases, to isolate, to exile somebody is to kill them, either quickly or slowly –'

'You mean,' I say, 'because they wouldn't have the means for survival?'

'Exactly. Well, nobody would, really. Even somebody who was going to go all survivalist, they're still going to be dependent on other people somehow. That exile and isolation are perceived as punishment – I think that must be absolutely hardwired into our brains – and that is, I think, how it must feel for so many people during lockdown, that somehow we are being rejected, punished, even shamed ...'

We are sitting in the 'Princes' Garden' of St Peter ad Vincula Church: a forbidding-looking Victorian affair of slate-clad tower and slate-strewn paths which occupies the middle of the village of Pennal, impeding the traffic of the main road. I am eating a Cadbury's Caramel. Jay is eating assorted nuts. By the north wall, among globular bushes, there is a bronze of Owain

Glyndŵr, the late-medieval prince and insurgent. He is depicted as a prototype all over again, all shaggy beard and lowering brow and not a trace of the regal pomp suggested by the image on his Great Seal. It is not the only way in which this place feels a little askew. Owain is said to have passed this way twice – he wrote a letter from Pennal in 1406, proposing terms for the support of France in his revolt against English rule – but that is the sum of the evidence that he was ever here. There is almost no historical substance to any of these crowding memorials: the statue, the garden, the painting inside the (locked) church showing 'the Welsh Assembly' held in the village, the various declarations that St Peter ad Vincula was 'Prince Owain Glyndŵr's Chapel Royal'. Rather, they are the doings of the rector here at Pennal between 1989 and 2012. A man named Geraint ap Iorwerth, he installed a Jewish menorah, a Qu'ran and statues of Shiva and the Buddha in his chancel and, notoriously, burnt several pages of the King James Bible as an 'artistic statement' before leaving his post to become an author, singer, screenwriter, inter-faith facilitator, novice shaman and professional masseur – or so it says on his LinkedIn page.

'Does lockdown feel that way to you?' I ask.

'It is really scary,' says Jay, 'especially going into winter. It's the first time I'll have had a winter in my house alone for a long time. I think it's going to be really unbearable unless I come up with a strategy . . . You know, my cat Otter, back in the spring, he was so close to me that there were several points when I thought, he's just going to start speaking little bits of English and I'm going to start speaking Felinese. Because he saw nobody, not even another cat. He had nothing and no one except me, and I had nothing and no one except him. Well. I saw my friend Marg once a week or something, but, well,' she laughs, 'it's not enough!'

I leave our bench, wander over radiating slates and crouch to consider one of four pierced stones – each, it seems, modelled on the Stone of Gronw, pierced by the spear of Lleu Llaw Gyffes in the 'Fourth Branch of the Mabinogi'. My admiration for Geraint ap Iorwerth increases by another increment. His Princes' Garden might have a whiff of the theme park, but it has all the gumption of Iolo Morganwg, the eighteenth–nineteenth-century poet and antiquarian whose passion for the culture and history of Wales overflowed into laudanum-fired invention – most famously, into Gorsedd Beirdd Ynys Prydain, the 'ancient' society of bards who first met on Primrose Hill in London in 1792 and whose colourful ceremonies remain a central part of the National Eisteddfod.

The cars continue to squeeze around us, plying between Machynlleth and Aberdyfi.

'One of the things,' says Jay, 'that has made me most upset with the whole Covid thing is the amount of energy that has been expended on stopping everything. Rightly. I mean, I'm very much pro-lockdown. But even so: stop exams, stop schools, stop work, stop football, stop the theatres, stop the pubs. Stop everything, *everything*, except the one thing that was actually responsible, the thing that caused the virus in the first place, which was our predatory attitude towards the living world. You might say it was just one bat, one virus hopping from a species to another, but actually it is an inevitable consequence of the destruction of habitats which derives from that predatory, invasive attitude ... I find it genuinely upsetting. There was a moment when we could have said, "We have to stop doing the things that cause these viruses to spread," and ...'

'We're dealing,' I say, 'entirely with the symptoms –'

'Yes. Yes. And it was barely discussed! All we've been able to talk about, all during Covid, has been human-to-human interactions, which are really important but are not the only thing. Going back to isolation, there is this whole other business of "species isolation": this idea humans have invented for themselves that simply discounts our relationship with everything else.'

'And it's a lie, fundamentally. I mean, people might isolate themselves from a group, but –'

'Yes, it is –'

'But, as a species, all you're actually doing is disguising from yourself the connection –'

'Oh!' Jay exclaims. 'Squirrel!'

This is the way of talking with Jay. However immersed she may be in a subject, she is always alert, always attending, and suddenly she will not be able to resist: this honeysuckle twining fragrant from a hedgerow; this oak as if with eyes and an elephant's trunk; this squirrel erect on the churchyard wall – and her excitement despite the fact that, not half an hour earlier, she devoted a good five minutes to squirrels' depredations of our native saplings.

We climb along the valley to the north of Pennal, trying to catch the leaves that shower from the beech trees, balancing over the stones in the streams. Here is a pile of shrink-wrapped silage. Here a sign warns of chalara ash dieback and phytophthora ramorum, counterparts of a sort to Covid-19. These imported diseases spell the end for most of our ash trees and our larch trees and, together with sweet chestnut blight and the oriental chestnut gall wasp, very likely our sweet chestnut trees too. We climb into the fields of Mynydd Cefn-caer, tacking through the rushes and the red-brown bracken while the aeroplanes continue to scrape across the sky. The gnarled slopes fall to the

Dyfi Valley – the river revealed now in that expanse, growing with each sky-coloured meander until it spreads in a bed of sand, drains into the dim grey sea. Already we are approaching the heights of the hills, deep-green, deep-red, there to the south. Already, their fence-line strung with little spruces, the fields are giving way to the uplands – to a track which cuts through the peat and shale, the white grass and the bilberry of yet another angular, sheep-stripped hilltop.

'The way I see it,' says Jay, 'part of the problem is the way that the climate crisis was first discussed by scientists. Not that their manner was inappropriate. It was right: dispassionate, cautious, impersonal ... But it was like that for decades. And I think what happened was that people in the media, people whose job it was to be messengers from the scientific community to the public, somehow felt that to have authority they had to speak in the same tone, when actually it was the worst thing that they could do.

'As a mammal, you just don't respond to danger in a cool, analytical manner. Faced with danger, any self-respecting meer-kat will show that they're alarmed. Which is what we didn't do. Instead, for years, we had an occasional news report, maybe twice a week on the BBC, with one person saying that climate change existed and a second person saying it didn't: a report employing the language of science and with no personal stories at all. And, meanwhile, we've had this entire narrative – well meant, but very misguided – which says, "Oh, you should always give people hope, you should never make people scared because fear paralyses." Well. In some moments, yes, extreme fear might feel paralysing, but for society as a whole it's necessary to be frightened by a threat of this magnitude. Look at Covid. Look at what happened there. The authorities were agreed that reporting something as frightening as a pandemic, in a frightening way, was the right thing to do. People were scared and, because of that, they acted ...'

'"Cautious optimism",' I say. 'That's the phrase that really gets me.'

'The whole David Attenborough thing,' says Jay. 'Well, it's not just him, of course, but his programmes are the obvious example. Don't misunderstand me, I think his work on climate change has been absolutely brilliant. I think it's been really bold of him to step forward as he has. But look at the narrative arc of one of his documentaries. You have forty-five minutes, say. You start really heavy with some heartbreaking images: you know, images of bats falling out of the trees, images of forest fires – and that feeling that these are the fires of hell ... So, people are watching those first scenes and images, and it's completely devastating, as it should be. But then, fairly quickly, the mood music gets less terrifying and soon it starts bubbling up into, you know, exactly that mood of "cautious optimism" and finally you reach: "It's possible that we can turn all this around." And the result is a very interesting and compelling piece of television. It's a really good story, but it's a story which finishes with "Let's have a cup of tea and forget about it because we don't have to go to bed scared."

'We've educated people into narcissism. We've educated people into this idea that we can have whatever we want, including peace of mind, when we're doing things that should mean that we forfeit our peace of mind. Actually to turn all this around, we have to be in a state of fear – or, we *would have had to be have been* in a state of fear, for long enough, long enough ago, for the change to have been effective ... If those programmes were left where we actually are, we would have been going to bed scared for years.'

Mynydd Rhyd-galed is a textbook watershed, complicated

by a minimum of life. Its ridge, which is wave-like, breaking to the north in a froth of shadow and exposed stone, rises behind us to conceal the River Dyfi and then to conceal all signs of the sea. In their place is the immense plantation promised by the periodic saplings: an endlessness of spruces, plus a few brown larches, in which our path soon disappears, in which the tracks run belligerently east to west. We are forced between the rows of trees – working backwards, keeping low to let our packs take the worst of the sharp, dead branches. It is enough to hold us both to silence for large parts of the afternoon. Now we arrive in a dell of a sort, its floor consumed by marsh hair moss so green as to appear luminescent. Now we meet a stream of pools and falls, its marshy banks crowded with colouring willows and brambles whose blackberries are all but gone. Now we scramble over a moss-swaddled wall, relic of the days not sixty years ago when this was still the province of sheep. Now we stumble into Bryn Eglwys Slate Quarry: spoil tips blurring with the fallen buildings; rails all but subsumed in the turf; a hole behind a wilting fence like the Lost World except inverted – its canopy of oaks and birches quite inaccessible to any creature except birds and insects.

These are no longer the long days of July. The thickening clouds are heavy with night when, weaving up the B4405 to avoid the cars and the thunderous lorries, Jay and I reach Cedris Farm. As it turns out, I have been complacent in my planning. The Dysynni Valley is a glaciated arch: a pair of bleak, monumental slopes, climbing to the crags that surmount each crest – each of them leaning, reaching forward, as if out of choice they would meet overhead. It is, in places, flanked by woods, but woods as steep as a flight of stairs, their scrubby oaks clinging to a

moss-caked scree which slips and clatters and defeats your boots
and lacks the level ground even of a sheep path. Cedris Farm,
on the other hand, has fields of soft and grazed-smooth grass
as flat as any river could provide, given sufficient millennia. It
is even a campsite, or so the sign says – even if the season has
plainly been and gone.

We hover, peer along the track, then venture to the house,
where a retired couple from the Midlands are enjoying a last
few days before the lockdown.

The mystery of what Jay's rucksack contains has been revealed
in parts throughout the day, when she has exchanged coats and
thermal vests in a series of complicated manoeuvres, when she
has produced maps and books, spare socks and an abundance
of health-giving foods. It is only, though, once we have erected
our tents, in the lee of a hedge beside the small, busy river,
that her possessions really start to emerge. Rain is slanting
from the south-west. She sits cross-legged in her vestibule, her
head-torch blazing, her top incisors resting on her bottom lip,
as they often will in concentration. She inflates a mat of decent
quality – unlike mine, which proves to have a leak. She arranges
pouches and Tupperware pots whose contents include: needle
and thread, a pencil sharpener, further honey-based snacks and
a sheaf of euros in readiness, perhaps, for a change of heart by
the British voting public. Then come a Trangia stove, tea bags,
pots, plates, cutlery, couscous and a vegetable curry. Then comes
a sleeping bag: a body of feathers and bright-orange fabric which
erupts from its sleeve and continues to expand until her face and
shoulders alone remain, close against the roof of the tent.

You start to think of Mary Poppins.

'£434!' she says.

Jay, I know, has always lived frugally. She survives on her
writing, which takes its own time, which has covered every

subject from rituals to childhood, twilight to wildness, and is no more given to compromise than anything else she does. At first I am unsure if I am expected to approve.

'That sleeping bag?' I ask, carefully.

'£434!' she repeats. 'I think that deserves a name.'

Her head-torch glancing from the strings of the rain, she carries her stove to the men's toilet block – a building, like the others, locked – whose door gives a sliver of shelter, and sets to work with oils and herbs.

'North Face of the Eider?' she suggests.

'Too cumbersome,' I say. 'It's very orange. How about Trump?'

A wind is mustering, pressing down the valley through the thin-leaved trees of the hedgerows and, audibly, the woods on those near-sheer slopes. It drags and rips at the flame of the stove. It twists and flails then carries off the rain and even tears the odd space in the cloud, so that stars show dimly, in brief, troubled patterns. It is on Jay's insistence that I abandon my tub of cold pasta and join her on the doorstep to share her curry, watching the hills, now giant silhouettes: black domes which reduce the sky, which require you to tip back your head, which flow seamlessly each into the next.

'Norman,' she says, in between mouthfuls.

'As in Lamont?'

'OK then. Herbie.'

'Why Herbie, for God's sake?'

'Well, he lies on the grass, doesn't he?'

'Do you not have a groundsheet?'

She stops, then frowns and eats again. 'Fox,' she decides, with satisfaction.

8

Cedris Farm to Dolgellau

20 October 2020

Tal-y-llyn is empty on this October morning, with lockdowns already in place in Conwy, Denbighshire, Wrexham and Flintshire, as well as most of the South Wales counties. Usually the hamlet must be something of a base camp for people climbing Cadair Idris. There are picnic tables beside Llyn Mwyngil: the lake which extends between the hulking hills, wrinkling, under the south-west wind, in the silvers of scree and the gingers of bracken, the greens of grass and the blacks, whites and fine, thin blues of the sky. Just across the lane is the Pen-y-Bont Hotel, its curtains drawn, a notice explaining the contingencies of Covid-19. A man in a plaster-spattered hoodie appears, scales a ladder and sets to work replacing a handful of slates on the roof. Just across the water is the Ty'n y Cornel Hotel – familiar, Jay and I realize together, from the television footage of the flooding in July. Even St Mary's Church, a fifteenth-century building prostrate to the cliffs of Mynydd Rugog, has been converted into 'a unique holiday experience'.

The path begins at the bottom of a beech wood: young, clear trunks pressed too close together, their auburn leaves gusting around us, suddenly fiery when a space of sunlight sweeps its way along the valley. A sharp turn right and we climb into pines – the wind carries upwards and carries the beech leaves to dance among their ranks of trunks – and so on to the open mountain, joining a track of broken stone. Here is the last of the farms, a place called Rhiwogof, its lambing sheds cut back into the slope. The house itself is clad in old grey concrete; the heads of its chimneys are rounded off, the better to dispel the rain. Inside its rough stone garden wall are plastic swings and a plastic slide, a trampoline and one or two plastic tractors – all of them drained of their once-bright colours. There is no extra income from tourists up here. There is nowhere to pitch a tent. The track continues, knits its way upwards into the brown, indigestible grass, its stone fading into the ruts of a quad bike. Long and lithe and low to the ground, a hare breaks from a tussock and flees for a gorse bush, hunching with his hind parts still clearly visible.

Rusting on a listing pole is the analogue television aerial you'll often find above the farms in the deeper valleys of Wales.

This is a landscape all about time. It is there in the thought of the ice that, just 20,000 years ago, carved the trench of the Dysynni Valley, lying to a depth of half a mile over all but the south-east fringe of Wales. It is there in the lake: that black-blue mile, small beneath our feet – the wind sending spasms along its back, tossing and shivering the oaks on its shore. Approaching on the road from Cedris Farm, you encounter, rising from the flat valley floor, a seeming range of miniature hills divided by fences and dry-stone walls, as if these are the same old fields. Their colour alone, a full vivid green, is enough to make you stop and scowl. Terminal moraine, I informed Jay – wrongly, as we can now see clearly. The green licks high up the far side of the valley, which itself recedes, must once have collapsed, damming the river, forming the lake.

And then, as we climb further still, a new stretch of the river appears in the west, snaking into low, rich fields, past a final cliff-framed crag. This is Craig yr Aderyn, a breeding site for choughs and peregrines, barn owls and redstarts, wheatears, linnets and cormorants – remarkably, being five miles from the sea. That jolt again: the gulf of time. From up here those fields look perfectly flat, with the lagoon in Tywyn shining dimly and the sea itself only an absence of land. It is nothing to imagine them covered in water – as, indeed, they would have been, before the drainage programmes of the eighteenth century, when Craig yr Aderyn overlooked the estuary.

The cormorants simply never left.

The coast of Wales is littered with such evidence of change. In some parts, like this, the sea has retreated. I remember, as a child, my attempts to make sense of the 'water gate' of Harlech Castle, to understand how the bay of the 1280s could possibly have become the Royal St David's Golf Club, dunes, caravans and a bird reserve: a spit, in fact, reaching almost to Porthmadog. But mostly the history is one of inundation.

Of Newgale Beach in 1171, Gerald of Wales writes:

The sandy shore of South Wales, being laid bare by the extraordinary violence of a storm, the surface of the earth, which had been covered for many ages, re-appeared, and discovered the trunks of trees cut off, standing in the very sea itself, the strokes of the hatchet appearing as if made only yesterday. The soil was very black, and the wood like ebony. By a wonderful revolution, the road for ships became impassable, and looked, not like a shore, but like a grove cut down, perhaps, at the time of the deluge . . .

Appearances of ancient tree stumps are almost a common occurrence these days, with the increased frequency and intensity of storms. This August, a whole new stretch was revealed at Llanrhystud by the ravages of Storm Francis – which, meanwhile, was destroying our tent in a field near St David's. It joined a list of almost seventy other sites where, periodically, stumps can be seen, from Rhyl and Abergele in the north, via Borth and Ynyslas in the west, to Whitesands Bay and Amroth in Pembrokeshire all the way to Goldcliff, east of Newport. Preserved, much as Gerald observes, in peat layers normally buried in sand, these are the relics of trees 5,000–6,000 years old – principally oak and pine, but willow, birch, alder and hazel as well. Other finds include the bones of long-vanished species, among them brown bear and aurochs, and, at Borth, a wattle walkway apparently constructed to deal with the steadily rising water.

That walkway marks the end of a very long process. During the Last Glacial Maximum, when most of Wales was under ice, the sea level was approximately 125 metres lower than it is today. The Irish Sea began to form in about 16000 BC but, as recently as 7000 BC, Cardigan Bay – the space between the Llŷn and the Pembrokeshire Peninsulas – remained dry and presumably inhabited, since it was around this time that the first post-Younger Dryas* settlers crossed from Britain to Ireland.

Such changes in land and sea have their echoes throughout Welsh culture, whether prompted by evidence like the exposed stumps or, as scholars will often suggest, by a folk memory of ancient catastrophe. In its account of Bendigeidfran's expedition to Ireland, the 'Second Branch of the Mabinogi'

---

* A period of cooling in the Northern Hemisphere, lasting from *c.* 10900–9700 BC

explains – astonishingly – that 'the sea was not wide then; Bendigeidfran waded across. There were only the rivers, the Lli and the Archan. Later the sea spread out when it flooded the kingdoms.' Nor is this the only reference – or possible reference – to sea level rise in *The Mabinogion*. Teithi Hen, in 'How Culhwch Won Olwen', is a king 'whose kingdom the sea overran, and he only just escaped and came to Arthur'. Caer Arianrhod, a castle in the 'Fourth Branch of the Mabinogi', shares its name with a reef about half a mile off the coast of Gwynedd, near the village of Llandwrog.

But these pale in comparison with Cantre'r Gwaelod. This is the legendary, low-lying realm ruled over by Gwyddno Garanhir (foster-grandfather of Taliesin) and defended by a dyke whose sluices permitted the draining of streams and rivers at low tide. According to the best-known version of the tale, dating from the sixteenth century, the keeper of the dyke was a drunkard named Seithenyn who, one evening, forgot about the changing tide and so allowed Cardigan Bay to overrun the kingdom, drowning all save the king himself. Its church bells, so the legend concludes, are still to be heard of an Aberdyfi evening: a feature, it seems, of many such stories. The same detail is to be found in the legend of Tyno Helig, which describes a land off the north coast of Wales, in the area of Colwyn Bay, ruled over by Helig ap Glannawg – until a curse is placed on his wicked daughter Gwendud and everything is swallowed by the sea. It is to be found in other traditions as well. It is said that the bells of the Breton city Ys – drowned under the Bay of Douarnenez after King Gradlon's wicked daughter Dahut caused the sluices of its dyke to be opened – are still to be heard on occasion. As are the bells of the town of Dunwich, lost to the erosion of the Suffolk coast. As are the bells of Nantgwyllt Church (in spite of the photographs of its demolition) beneath Caban Coch Reservoir in the Elan Valley, back south in the Cambrian Mountains.

Such is the accretion of legend.

The first recorded version of the legend of Cantre'r Gwaelod is to be found in the thirteenth-century *Black Book of Carmarthen*. A poem named 'Boddi Maes Gwyddno' ('The Drowning of the Lands of Gwyddno'), it laments the negligence of a well-maiden, Mererid, who allows her well to overflow and so to flood the entire land – raising the fascinating possibility that, since water marks the boundary between two worlds, the encroachment of the sea was seen as nothing less than an encroachment by the Otherworld.

Sunlight spears from the clouds to the south, casting patches of translucent colour into a greyness marked, if you peer closely, by the windmills of the Cambrian Mountains. The colour advances patiently, begins to illuminate bands of that landscape far beyond the Dyfi Estuary: the dome of a hill, a snaring valley, an escarpment, a pocket of trees. It is hard to believe that it is the same wind at work. What there seems patience, here is hysteria; the tawny tufts of the Molinia grass are churning as if they were sea anemones. Jay and I continue to climb, at the slow, steady pace that comes with hours. We are following – still – the ruts of the quad bike, although these are slopes which, back in the Cambrians, would surely be thought fit only for a horse. Quads can be treacherous. Quads tend to roll. Even now, when June comes round and the Elan Valley farmers combine forces to gather in their hefted flocks, they will ride only horses for a full two weeks – to Llyn Teifi, Drygarn Fawr, Allt y Ddinas, Esgair Wen.

The quad ruts vanish only with the pelt of the soil, where the rocks become like armoured plates, where the scree lies in patterns like light on water. The wind has us shouting to one another. We are all but crawling, inching upwards. We have shared out, for now, Jay's weightier possessions, but even so she is twice thrown from her feet. We cross the neck of a ridge, 1,000 feet above the vast, gouged space which contains Llyn Cau – its water, as dark as lead, erupting into flashes of white. We find ourselves among paths dividing, fanning over the wreckage of Penygadair, each one seeking out the way in the bawling wind, beneath the black, hanging cloud – one path scrambling across the loose stone, another worming far to the left where an outcrop might give a serviceable foothold.

Penygadair, the summit, is the landscape in essence. The slightest scraps of a yellow-brown grass are all that contend with its slicing spurs, its bare, square hut, its scummy pools, its quartz-flecked rocks. In one cleft, a man is eating a pie. For our part, Jay and I come north of the trig point before we sit and listen to the air that sings and shrieks above and around us, ringing with that and with the weightless feeling that comes from dispensing with your rucksack. Past the lip beyond our feet, Gwynedd is a disarray of clouds and light to a distance we cannot apprehend, of streams drawn by their lines of trees, of lumpish hills and forestry – all of them converging on that next, west-flowing river, the Mawddach: a grey-blue banner, ever dilating, while the land at last submits to the sea.

On the south shore of the estuary is Fairbourne: the first village in Britain, notoriously, expected to be lost to climate change.

*

'I was part of the SMP,' says Claire Earlie, 'the Shoreline Management Plan. Do you know about that? Basically it's a document that sets out the map, if you like, of the next hundred years *of how we'd like to manage the coastline. It's a beefy document. It took years to write. The whole of the UK coastline is split up into these sections, so, for instance, you'll have one from St Anne's Head in Pembrokeshire, past Swansea and Carmarthen and all the way in to the Severn Estuary. And we'd look at everything on the coast – not just property and infrastructure. We'd look at communities. We'd look at environmental designations. Then we'd do modelling for different scenarios, different sea level rise scenarios based on the IPCC reports. We'd take a digital model of the elevation of the land, and we'd say, right, what would happen if we cast different water levels on top of that? And then if we add waves? What if we have a joint probability analysis, when you've got a spring high tide and a storm surge and six-metre waves and a one-metre sea level rise? If we look at the worst-case scenarios, what would happen? You have so many possibilities.'*

Dr Earlie is a Lecturer in Coastal Processes, a colleague of Marie Ekström in the School of Earth and Environmental Sciences at Cardiff University. This is August 2021, and she is speaking to me from her home in Penarth, where she grew up and which she left as a teenager, expecting never to return – though Penarth is woven into her voice, sounding in all of the local place names, and you could hardly expect her to live inland. She is a daily swimmer-in-the-sea, a 'wave fanatic' by her own definition.

'You have these four scenarios, these four choices,' she explains. 'First is "hold the line", which means maintain the current defences; then you have do nothing, or "no active intervention" as it's called; then there's "managed realignment", which is where you work with nature and realign the coast to allow a bit of space; and finally there's "advance the line", which is moving towards the coast, creating land, which is really rare. For argument's sake, you might say Dubai is advance the line. Cardiff would be hold the line. No matter what, we hold the line . . . But this was

SMP2 – they'd already done SMP1 about ten years earlier – and SMP2 took a different approach. We weren't just asking, how do we get through the next hundred years? We were asking, how do we get to a point in a hundred years' time when we're not handing on problems to the next generation? So, if you like, it's kind of a stepped approach ... We were just providing expert opinion – it's not statutory – but that's where Fairbourne's decision would have come from.'

'How would you characterize the Fairbourne decision, then?' I ask. 'Because, well, the term "decommission" is –'

'A difficult one.'

'Yeah ...'

'I know. "Decommission", like it's a factory or something ... You have to be so careful with that sort of language, because these are people's homes, and people's dreams to move there ...' Claire drops her eyes for a moment. 'One of the key things about SMP2 that Greg Guthrie and I tried to do, back in 2008, 2009, was to get the communities involved and show them the science, and say, this is what's going to happen. We cannot change it. We cannot build a wall in front of the town, because then you're actually losing the very thing you're trying to maintain. Your coastal town would no longer be a coastal town, it would just have a big wall in front of it.'

'It's already,' I say, 'got something of a wall in front of it.'

'Well, exactly. It's already pretty grim. You can't really see the sea so much ... The thing with Fairbourne is that it's surrounded by hills and it's really low-lying. It's flat. It's pretty much at the high-water mark. So if you have a big storm and loads of rain falling in the mountains then you already have an issue with drainage, but then you have, say, a spring high tide and a big storm surge on top of that of forty, fifty centimetres, and then you chuck a few metres of waves on top of that ... Well, you could

*easily breach those defences, and once that happens, you've got
an area of land that becomes a giant puddle. You see, it's not
just a question of the sea level – though the projections are that,'
she gives a grim laugh, 'that's really going to go up. If you get a
big enough storm that breaches the defences, that's it. Over, in
seconds. And that is the message that I think is being missed
when it comes to understanding why we can't defend a place like
Fairbourne. Because the storms are going to be getting more and
more frequent and more and more intense, and there's only so
much concrete that you can keep pouring . . .*

'Anyway,' Claire says, returning to her subject. 'The SMP works
on a timescale of a hundred years, divided up into "epochs": zero
to twenty years, then twenty to fifty years, and then fifty to a hundred years. The decision with Fairbourne for this first epoch was:
do nothing, no active intervention. Whereas there will be other
places, like Amroth, which are "hold the line" for this epoch,
then in the next epoch you're starting to move towards managed
realignment. But, in fifty years' time, it's going to be very difficult
to keep defending these villages like Fairbourne, Borth, Ynyslas,
Dale . . . It's not just the physics, there's finance involved as well.
There's this pot of money designated to coastal protection and
it isn't very big and 60 per cent of people in Wales live on the
coast. I've lain awake at night just thinking, God, there's going to
be all of these places gone. In some cases, managed realignment
will work. If you make a bit of space, and allow these natural
buffers to work: the beach, sand dunes, cliffs, shingle barriers,
salt marshes, mud flats, these are all natural sea defences that
dissipate wave energy before it reaches the land. Little Haven,
for example, has been managed realignment. They've moved the
car park back and made a bit of space. There's a few little places
around Wales where they've done that, and it's quite effective.
But obviously it comes with the loss of homes and in some places,*

like Fairbourne, with the mountains behind it, they can't retreat.
There's nowhere to go.'

'One thing I have to ask about,' I say. 'If you look at the projections provided by Climate Central or by UKCP18 from the Met Office, you really don't need much sea level rise before key bits of infrastructure start experiencing major problems. Given the hills, the roads and railways do tend to run very close to the coastline. And it's really, really difficult to see where else they could go. Like, the M4 between the Severn Estuary and Newport, or the railway line running up the Gwynedd Coast . . .'

'It's crazy, isn't it?' Claire both nods and shakes her head. 'And even the stretch of railway in Ferryside, opposite Llansteffan – that's a really key stretch. Actually it's where my parents live. I don't know if you've ever been on the train to Pembroke or Milford Haven, but the line is right there, right on the coast . . . And I don't know what they're going to do about it. I think it might just end up being a game of whack-a-mole. They'll solve one problem at a time, when they're faced with it. I mean, if we were to sit down, all the engineers in Wales and think, right, what can we do? How much would it cost to move or maintain this infrastructure? Well, I just don't think the money is there. And that's why the SMP has this step-by-step approach, saying that this stretch of the coastline is quite at-risk, so maybe we maintain it for the next fifty years and then we think about a strategy to maybe start moving things inland a bit . . . But there is plenty of time.'

'Well,' I say, 'so long as people are doing something.'

'Yes. Not just ignoring it for a hundred years . . .'

'So what do we do?' I ask. 'How do we respond to all of this?'

'We've got to realize,' says Claire, 'that we cannot stop this happening, despite what we can do to reduce it, and I think that for many people who live at the coast, who want to live at the coast and want it to be there forever, there's a lot of denial. Sea levels *are going to keep rising because of global warming, because if you heat up water it expands and because ice loss is inputting more water into the system. And then there's the increase in frequency and also intensity of storms. Just last week, my swimming friends were taking photos and videos of waves crashing up over the sea wall on to the Promenade ... The policy for Penarth is hold the line, I think. But it's another of those places where you can't retreat. There's a big cliff behind it. You have to think, what will happen? And if we get more southerly-tracked storms, which we might ... Do you remember the winter of 2013–14? I was doing my PhD in Plymouth at the time, and I was studying storms around the south-west of Cornwall, and that was incredible. Typically you get westerly and south-westerly, north-westerly Atlantic storms, but that winter we had so many storms that shifted south. There were loads of places around Newquay and all around the Cornish coastline that were completely smashed to bits by the waves.'*

'It can sound ridiculous to me,' I say, 'sometimes, to be worrying about a village like Broad Haven when, in Bangladesh, you have something in the way of 100,000 people a year already being displaced by sea level rise. The thing is, I suppose, that this is our home. And that's the same for everyone, wherever they are. This is our home, and so it's important to us, and it's important as well that people have some understanding that these are changes that we're going to have to come to terms with. It's important that we have an open conversation so that people can, if they have to, start to grieve.'

'Yes,' says Claire. 'Yes, exactly. I think a lot about the little villages, like Ferryside and Llansteffan and Broad Haven and Porthdinllaen: places that are all in the SMP. And I just don't know how we're going to keep hold of them. These little places, I think, they're as important as the big places. From the perspective that people live there, of course, but also because they're part of *what makes Wales Wales. And I think that's the thing that people in Fairbourne are pissed off about. It feels to many people that it's just been a decision that's been imposed on them. They've been part of the consultation process, but there's a feeling that "they're doing this to us". Whereas I think it needs to be: we're all affected, if you have any compassion for humans at all.'*

*

'I went to Fairbourne the other day,' says Jay. 'I took my godson on the miniature railway.'

'Go on then,' I say, digging out my pasta. 'What's it like?'

'I think,' she says, after several moments and apparently in answer to a different question. She works on a mouthful of colourful leaves. 'I think most people are inherently good. I think most people believe good of others. I think that, when most people go to the supermarket to buy their slab of beef or their chocolate bar, they assume such things are not a result of tearing down the Amazon or the rainforests of West Papua. They assume that their £5 T-shirt from Peacocks is not a result of child exploitation ... What can I say? Fairbourne is a crazy place. It's so low-lying, you can hardly believe it exists, even now. But the estate agents give a value to its houses and, by and large, I think we just trust them. To us that means that they must be safe ...'

Jay and I met in 2013 when, along with the novelist Toby Litt, we shared a stage in a tent at Hay Festival. We were among the contributors to a book called *Beacons*: a collection of stories envisioning futures under climate change – although, in fact, my story was set in Iron Age Radnorshire and most of the other writers had an equally loose interpretation of the rules. If this gives an impression of years devoted to fathoming the best way to write about climate, then for Jay at least it is accurate enough.

In those years, I was largely changing nappies, soothing fears in the middle of the night and trying with the one hand to deal with a crippling relationship crisis and with the other to scratch a living at the South Wales universities. But Jay was the writer in residence at the Potsdam Institute for Climate Impact Research. She was working with the organization Tipping Point to communicate to the public the depth and the urgency of the climate crisis. Long before it had crossed my mind, she was coming to terms with the need, as she writes in *This Is Not a Drill*, 'to put oneself on the line, because words (and this is a heavy heresy for a writer) are not enough'.

Walking with Jay is a basic sanity. It has a sense almost of deliverance when your life has become so much defined by a tension, by the irreconcilability between the apparent reality of daily experience, of its reflection in the media, its reflection in politics, and the reality of scientific fact. Two people are able to generate a culture, and our culture here, as we emerge from our shelter, strap on our rucksacks and pull down our hats, is one at least receptive to the science – as, to be honest, I have not always been. In fact, for many years I made every effort to avoid any information relating to climate or ecology, living instead with an obscure anxiety. Which is, I suspect, quite a common condition.

We creep down a scree, between precipitous drops, looking down on Llyn y Gadair, an almost-oval of turbulent water, its surface alive with figures of spray, with shapes like fronds, with shapes like spirits.

If you stand on the corner of a Cardiff street and attempt to engage people on the subject of climate change, you will tend to receive one of five reactions. Many people, of course, go hurrying past, chatting or else with their eyes on a phone or on some patch of the pavement ahead. Almost all will keep their distance – some expressing support with a couple of words or perhaps a lifted thumb, others (occasionally) spitting out abuse: 'Get a fucking job' or 'Get a fucking bath'. Still, scores of people will stop and talk. Of these, probably the larger part are those who have, essentially, no notion of the climate emergency, those who reveal in the starkest terms the absolute failure of our government and public-service media. 'Serious?' they ask, as you make efforts to explain. 'Serious?' And then you have the group that for several years, had I had the courage to stop at all, probably would have included me. These are the people who will take a flyer, express support but in the same breath regret that, having small children, having this or that job or responsibility, it is simply too much for them to engage. Perhaps there is something here of Jay's thoughts on Fairbourne. Perhaps these are people who, in the end, trust that our governments have things in hand. Perhaps, being inherently good, they simply cannot believe that human beings could wreak such devastation as the scientists project. To speak for myself, mine was a type of denial, not of fact but of extent. It was a sense that life was hard enough, that the last thing I needed was yet another problem – even if this problem is the *sine qua non*, the problem on which all other problems depend.

9

Dolgellau to Llyn Cynwch

28 May 2021

Illtyd, as depicted in the west window of Llanelltyd Church, Dolgellau, is the full Galahadian hero: a young man in silver armour, a long sword in one hand, the lance in the other flying a banner the colour of bluebells. His hair is golden within his halo. A pair of angels hover with his helmet. As an image, it is at once absurd and exact. Llanelltyd is Illtyd's only dedication anywhere to be found in North Wales. Either he or one of his acolytes must have followed the Western Seaways, ventured into the Mawddach Estuary and founded this church in the wilds of the hinterland, far outside the saint's usual *patria*. Even these days, North and South Wales can feel very much like separate countries, and that this difference existed all of 1,500 years ago is evident just from the name of the place. Illtyd's south-coast monastery is commonly known as Llantwit Major – twit being a corruption of -iltuath, the Goedelic version of his name, reflecting an Irish cultural presence. Here in North Wales, Llanelltyd retains the Brittonic form -elltyd, as befits a region more purely

British, and the more so after the early 400s A D, when the Old North chieftain Cunedda purged Gwynedd of its Irish colonists. It was in the nature of the early saints to set off into unknown parts, to take the fight to the powers of darkness in the desert, in the wilderness – and here is at least one of the ways in which the military and sacred were aligned at this time. By the beginning of the fourth century, the Christians of the Roman Empire were no longer facing persecution. The martyrs would, of course, remain an inspiration, but it was the wandering ascetics who were the new heroes of the Christian world.

Like so many of the churches in Wales, Llanelltyd Church is barn-like, low with heavy beams. Its walls are white. Its pews are oak. With an overcast evening in the deep-sunk windows, it is a struggle to make out the various notices – this one concerns Covid-19, this one the funeral hatchment of Sir Robert Vaughan of Nannau – and yet it would feel wrong to turn on the lights. Despite the neighbouring A470, somehow the place has its own composure, a sense of silence not to be profaned. Perhaps it is simply a matter of history, a quality born out of centuries of worship, out of all that iterated meaning. I pass back through the arch of the porch, wave to the man at Tandalar, the B&B across the road, who kindly agreed to stretch a point and unlock this heavy door, and stand again among the tall, splaying yew trees in the raised and circular *llan*, or churchyard. Certainly, Llanelltyd is an ancient site – although how ancient is more or less guesswork. By and large, the saints sought virgin territory – fresh points of connection between themselves and God – but often too they would repurpose spaces of an existing significance. Here, in this churchyard, the stoutest of the yews has a girth of thirty feet, suggesting an age of 1,500 or even 2,000 years. It might have been planted by Illtyd himself. It might have been here for half a millennium before he was even born. Such churchyards as Defynnog in Breconshire, Discoed in Radnorshire, Bettws Newydd in Monmouthshire and Llangernyw in Conwy give clearer examples of extreme age. In these you will find yews very much broader, although often fragmented, so that the Llangernyw Yew, at thirty-five and a half feet, might conceivably be 5,000 years old – older than most of Wales's prehistoric monuments.

The saints were rarely evangelists; they were not looking to improve the world so much as to spurn its evil. Their goal, it seems, was 'passionlessness': a condition, acquired by meditation and ascetical self-discipline, in which the mind would be free fully to contemplate God. '[By] this ordering of daily life,' so St Anthony explained, 'we shall neither fall into sin, nor have a lust for anything, nor cherish wrath against any, nor shall we heap up treasure on earth.' All the same, the saints were not Egyptians; they comprehended these Eastern principles by means of their own Celtic structures. When you couple this with inculturation – the adaptation of the Christian liturgy, without which the religion cannot hope to take root in any non-Christian cultural background – inevitably, the result is a hybrid. The saints inhabited a Christian culture, but one with an emphasis on severed heads and on the central role of the poet; one drawn to yew trees, stones and wells; one whose saints, and there were many hundreds, were figures of purportedly magical abilities, often belonging to long, heroic lineages, each with his or her local sphere of influence – each, in fact, hardly to be distinguished from the regional deity going before.

Such was the culture that became Wales. Picture one of the early saints: a man most likely, probably alone, in sandals of hide and a monkish habit without a hood to guard his head. He is struggling through an Iron Age landscape of solitary farmsteads, marshes and mountains, a pack suspended from his bony shoulders containing a little food, a cup and skin-bound books for Mass and Office. He will sleep outside or in some barn, begging his way in exchange for a blessing. He will drop at last into some forested valley – there to find and found his *llan*, to build a cell of mud and wattle, to raise a preaching cross. In the end, there were more of these *llannau* – these Celtic Christian sites – than Wales was ever able to digest. Some 44 per cent of them remain in their original isolation. But most attracted a house or two as the new (or reborn) religion spread, as the population shifted from the hills to the valleys, as the cells of the saints were rebuilt as churches, first in timber, then in stone – becoming the nuclei of the pattern of settlement that is the map of Wales today. It is a pattern to madden any civil engineer, having scant consideration for agriculture or trading routes or other demands of the physical environment – its original impulse being seclusion, wildness and awe.

'It is,' writes the ecclesiologist T. J. Hughes, 'an upturning of the order of things – a pattern of settlement in reverse, where the sacred has a generative role.'

On the far side of the River Mawddach, its green, hurried water and banks of pebbles, a lane passes lines of bright dome tents, camper vans with windscreen covers, static caravans with their own neat hedges, barbecues issuing fatty smoke around the striped tarpaulin windbreaks. Two small boys are pursuing a football. The adults, trailed by or trailing a dog, smile without face masks, offer their greetings, give off all of the warmth and pleasure of human society all but restored. The lane leads to a farmhouse and a cluster of barns where a couple are leaning on a stable door, talking the unfamiliar Welsh of the North. Beside them are the ruins of Cymer Abbey: foundations dividing a small, trim field, turning through buttercups, turning again to join the ragged, standing walls.

A blackbird gives his questioning call.

A mouse flits past me and into a hole.

The Cistercians, a monastic order established in 1098 at Cîteaux Abbey in eastern France, found their way to Wales in the early twelfth century, founding a first house at Tintern, Monmouthshire, in 1131. Their success here, in retrospect, looks like a given. With the centuries following the Age of Saints defined by isolation and religious intransigence, then by the sudden upheaval of the Norman Conquest – the Norman imposition of parishes and dioceses, their destruction of the traditional *clas* system – the Cistercians must have seemed to be providing a return to the original forms of Welsh monasticism. They were committed to asceticism and to remote, inhospitable sites. Among the best-known reflections of Bernard of Clairvaux, perhaps their most influential figure, is that 'You will find something more in woods than in books. Trees and stones will teach you that which you can never learn from masters.'

Again like the saints, the Cistercians owed much of their success to the ways in which they engaged with the landscape and traditions of Wales. A few years back, I was fortunate enough to spend a weekend with a group of experts at Strata Florida, the Cistercian abbey near Pontrhydfendigaid, once a rival in importance to St David's Cathedral. Leading us among the ruins of the Abbey Church, Professor David Austin stopped before the site of the high altar, the heart of the monastery's ritual practice. Here two sets of steps lead into a cistern: a holy well whose off-true alignment, as confirmed by a recent resistivity survey, is that of an earlier monastery. Formerly, Professor Austin explained, the well was fed – via conduit – by another holy well. This was one of several near the head of the 'sacred' Glasffrwd Valley, a group enclosed by a 'remarkable' collection of twenty-six Bronze Age monuments and met, out of the Cambrian Mountains, by an ancient route of pilgrimage.

Unlike Cîteaux Abbey, Strata Florida was not built in a 'wilderness ... where men rarely penetrated and none but wild things lived'. It was built in a place whose sacred significance had stood for millennia.

For all of which, on this late-May evening, it is easy to see how Llanelltyd would appeal – to Illtyd or his acolyte in the sixth century, to the Cistercian monks in the twelfth. There is a grandeur to the county of Gwynedd, a depth to its valleys, a scale to its mountains quite distinct from anywhere further to the south. Trees clothe sheer and mist-smeared slopes. A field or so distant, the River Mawddach opens on its startling estuarine plain. Leaving the lane near a farm named Garth-bleiddyn, I scramble up a shaley track, mud and runnels sucking at my boots. It has not just been lockdown that has kept me from Sarn Helen: Wales has seen its wettest May on record, pushing 1967 into second place by a comprehensive 30 per cent. For now, though, the rain has stopped. The year is revealed in its early-summer rapture. The verges, viewed from a certain angle, present only a flush of colour: red campion, buttercups, speedwell, stitchwort, bluebells teetering almost into violet. In the fields, the hawthorns are bodies of white. For the first time, I realize, since leaving Neath, there is no discernible noise of an aircraft. The flight paths, apparently, lie to the south. It is like being freed from chronic pain. And there, as a lake, Llyn Cynwch, appears from the brown-tipped rushes and the crozier bracken that crest another slope, a cuckoo is calling just as he used to. Even my mother, a cuckoo fanatic, has rarely heard them in our parts for years.

One cuckoo. Another cuckoo. I have barely arrived in this small, high valley and squatted down beside the lake – its mirror of oaks and scree-scattered hilltops – when a second voice starts on the opposite hillside.

Over several minutes, they move into phase and then move apart again.

It is hypnotic. It is disconcerting, like encountering somebody dead in a dream.

The early saints are masked by time; it can be hard to grasp any sense of their reality. Their cells have long ago rotted away. Their *Lives* contain little more than scraps, buried among the angelic prophecies, the fatal curses and encounters with the devil. All the same, there are odd moments when they seem to appear through the veils of legend. To begin with, there is their context. Theirs was an age of continual adversity: the long decline of the Roman Empire, the Irish and Anglo-Saxon invasions, the Yellow Plague of the middle sixth century, which probably killed Maelgwn Gwynedd and, despite its description in the *Life* of St Teilo, probably did not present as 'a column, consisting of a watery cloud passing over the whole region'. As these men (almost all of them men) forsook the evils of the world, they were shunning corruption and entrenched inequality. They were seeking to confirm their heroic manhood or to atone for some grievous sin, but they were also, sometimes, fleeing for their lives – as St Samson, in the years of plague, escaped to Dol in Brittany. And then they can be known as a class. With scarcely an exception, these were no inspired peasants. These were the children of royalty, or of aristocrats at the very least – frequently, a younger son. They were young, educated, idealistic. Paul Aurelian, for example, as he is described in Wrmonoc's ninth-century *Life*, rebelled against his father, a Romano-British chieftain, and left as a monk to establish his cell 'in a secluded place adjoining his father's possessions'.

One eye, perhaps, was on those left behind.

Above all, there are their places. On the slope above the lake
I gulp down my pasta, along with a couple of mouthfuls of
Talisker, and lay my mat beside an oak alive but so long fallen
that all of its branches are vertical. I walk the short way around
the nose of the hill: an Iron Age fort, as the map confirms, by
the name of Foel Faner. A greater spotted woodpecker lands
on a rock, gives one shrill and looks around. The calls of the
cuckoos are once more converging, although they soon fade
into the A470. There is the abbey. There is the church. There,
beneath a fracturing, blue-silver sky, beneath the cloud-crowned
mass of Cadair Idris, the mountain Jay and I descended seven
months ago now, beneath the wooded and hard, torn slopes,
the River Mawddach wanders through fertile fields, marshes
and sandbanks, which gather to a spit and so into Fairbourne:
land which, according to the projections, will all of it soon have
been taken by the waves. But for now, essentially, this remains
the landscape Illtyd knew. On this motionless, early-summer
evening of cuckoos and delicate, new-burst leaves, of distant
cattle and the open sea, it is lovely enough to stop your breath.

10

Llyn Cynwch to
Maenofferen Slate Quarry

29 May 2021

If, ultimately, Wales exists because the alternative was too much hassle – the border being the edge of the hard, wet hills, where the Anglo-Saxons looked at one another and decided to consolidate – then Gwynedd is its apotheosis. Gwynedd is a fortress in itself; it was born for the guerrilla tactics that, in the 50s AD, the Silures visited on the Roman legions and, in the 1400s, Owain Glyndŵr visited on Henry IV. Look from the brink of this high, thin path, down across the near-sheer heather and the hawthorns whose blossom is coming only now, and you look into a Mawddach Valley showing no sign of the imminent sea: a trench, it seems, cut equally by that grey and constrained river and by that grey and constrained road. It is a scene even the Climate Change Committee could scarcely amend. The valley floor is a ribbon of interlocking fields, each one the inside of a meander. The sides are mostly larch plantations the deep red-orange of last year's bracken, plus bands of spruce and deciduous trees so green as to be almost fluorescent. The tops are the mountains, bare and brown and patrolled by one or two discernible sheep. Their Grade 5 – 'very poor-quality' – land dominates the landscape, as it does the maps of the North.

Ludicrously, far below, a big white car overtakes a small red car.

Their noise rises like the rushing of a sea.

Like the Dyfi Valley farmer said, the Precipice Walk is quite a thing – if it is less precipice than very steep slope. It weaves along this easterly hillside, 800 feet or so above the river, through fresh green bilberry, stretching bracken and the scrubby little trees of the *ffriddoedd*: these borders to the open hills called 'sidelands' back in Radnorshire. This early in the morning the path is deserted except for a cuckoo, which calls a while then crosses the slope like some ungainly falcon. Again, with the green earth and with the grey sky, there is a feeling that this is Wales as it was, Wales as it ought to be.

A mile passes.

Another mile.

The path forks in a hush of drizzle. After some moments of squinting at the map, I weave downhill into mobs of birch – into the 9,000 acres of a wood, Coed y Brenin.

*

'The wildwood,' says Mary Gagen. 'It's impossible not to be intrigued by that, isn't it? This idea of the pre-Neolithic mixed deciduous woodland that would have covered the UK. Though, actually, the research suggests that it was more open than we often think. When you look at the pollen record from lakes at that time, there is far more grassland pollen than you'd expect if the wood-land was dense. And anyway, given our latitude and how wet our

climate is, it makes far more sense for there to have been small areas that were open pastureland and open grassland. I always imagine, if you were living in that landscape, you would have looked at those open patches and thought, this is where I can settle and raise sheep. It's natural to have thought, let's expand on that.

'But yes, we've now lost about half the native species that were here, just because we have been messing with the landscape for 6,000 years.'

Mary is a Professor of Geography at Swansea University: a specialist in climate change, tree ring science, palaeoclimate, carbon isotopes and a number of other related areas.

We are speaking on Zoom in early May 2021.

'In the Cambrian Mountains,' I say, 'I'd talk to people sometimes about cutting peat, back in the days when you were allowed to do that. They would dig up these birch trees and use them for kindling.'

'Those peat sediments will probably have been much, much older than the Neolithic,' Mary says. 'They'd be going back to the Younger Dryas: this period when there was this small, weird advancement of the glaciation, 11,000 years ago or so. The Younger Dryas boundary – it's a pale layer in the peat sediments in Wales, and below that boundary the peat is much older. That kind of cold birch woodland would have been post-glacial rather than Neolithic. You can imagine what Sweden and Finland look like now, with silver birch forest stretching for miles, and the trees quite small?

'As for the oldest woodland we have today,' she goes on, with barely a breath, 'that falls into two types, really: ancient oak woodland and temperate Celtic rainforest. Have you come across that as a biome? It's basically a peculiarity: ancient oak woodlands in river valleys. The reason they form is to do with the amount of moisture in the air. The splash-back from rivers is *critical because it allows the lower plants – the bryophytes and the liverworts and the mosses – to grow on the trunks of the trees. It's not the trees that are most important in temperate rainforest, it's those lower plant forms. So ... they're not rainforests in the Amazonian sense – they're not seeding their own monsoonal cloud systems – but we refer to them as rainforest, partly, I suppose, because it sounds good, but also in recognition of their mildness and of the fact that the water is critically important to their being there.'*

'And these are the sort of trees you study in your dendroclimatological work?' I ask.

'Well, that side of it is really the work of Neil Loader and other colleagues.'

'Could you give an overview?'

Mary considers. 'Really, it's a 900-year record of how wet our summers have been in Wales and England. Most people know that you can look at the width of the ring in a tree trunk and that tells you what the climate was like, but you can also look at the changes in the chemistry of the wood from year to year, and in particular – it's what we specialize in at Swansea – you can analyse oxygen isotopes. It's quite a revealing bit of research, really, because you can tie a really bad summer, or a bunch of really bad summers, with the archaeological and historical records of famines. For example, the "agrarian crisis" of the early fourteenth century. Or the 1430s, which was the most severe famine of the fifteenth century. Really, you see this terrifying record of how much we have relied, historically, on stability in our climate. We're looking into the past to see the future. I think a lot of people think that global warming is just that, that it will be hotter and drier. Obviously it isn't – it's more extremes – so in Wales in particular we can expect a lot of very, very wet summers and winters and the crop failures that accompany that will cause food issues. We're not future-proofed from that. We still could really, really suffer . . .

'Wales we always call a perfect living lab, because of its size and its accessibility and its diversity. It's got all these features which make it a great little microcosm. You can get your head around Wales, when a lot of this stuff can be just overwhelming. And particularly in terms of managing woodland it's got a very interesting and useful history, because we took all our woodland away – or almost all – and then we tried to replant some, and we screwed that up, and then everyone was so disheartened that we virtually stopped planting altogether. So you can study all those problems.'

'We screwed that up,' I say. 'Can you explain?'

'What I had in mind was when we planted swathes of Japanese larch, and many of them died from [the tree disease] phytophthora. Farmers can be very reticent now if you talk to them about woodland creation on their land – a lot of farmers really bought into that planting scheme – and . . . you can't ignore that cultural perspective. The fact is, a significant quantity of Welsh people do not want woodland – they want agricultural land with a few sheep on it. That's what we think Wales looks like – that's our heritage, our cultural memory – and I fully sympathize with that attitude. Nevertheless, we need to plant trees. The new State of the UK's Woods and Trees *report is just terrifying. Something like only 7 per cent of UK woodlands are in a healthy condition, and we are so far behind on planting. Wales is committed to planting, I think, 2,000 hectares of woodland a year and last year we planted eighty. It's just woeful.'*

'And the CCC recommends 180,000 hectares,' I say. 'How on earth could we hope to manage that?'

'Well . . .' Mary says. 'Do you know about the National Forest for Wales, first of all?'

'Go on. What's the situation with that?'

'*The situation is that there was a big flashy announcement, people like me got pedalled out and plastered all over the government's webpages and the* Guardian *and it was all very exciting. And then there was a pandemic . . . What I like about the National Forest for Wales plan is that it looks basically at connectivity – at identifying ancient patches of woodland and figuring out how to "corridor" them, how to connect them. And there can be really big wins with things like that, particularly in terms of protecting wildlife and ecosystem services. But there's a limit to how much even a scheme like this can do . . . I know ancient woodland's our greatest possession, but it's already protected and it's a tiny percentage – about 4.5 per cent of Wales. In order to thrive, it really just needs us to shut the door and keep humans out. Instead we need to be focusing on the scrublands: the little patches of degraded woodland. How do you make them part of a working landscape that can contribute to the low-carbon economy? How do you make them healthy in terms of biodiversity, in terms of carbon, in terms of flood reduction? No one's doing that experiment. We're obsessed with woodland creation on pasture, and preservation of our ancient woodland, but if we leave the scrublands out of the connectivity corridor we're not going to be able to achieve what we want.*'

'*What do we want, then? What are our priorities?*'

Mary gives one of those laughs. '*There's not really a hierarchy of issues any more, it's a bombarding circle of pressures, and we really can't ignore any of them. If you want to lay down carbon, the best thing is a hideous, monoculture spruce plantation – though you're only going to get significant lay down in the trunks after thirty years or so. We need that sort of fast-growing softwood timber. There's not really any getting away from that. We need to stop building with concrete and steel and start building with wood again. We've also got to deal with the fact that we have biosecurity issues with importing wood, so we need to start growing our own for that reason too. But, basically, any plan has got to be far-reaching. It can't just be: let's worry about the ancient woodland, ignore plantation and ignore parkland and ignore urban trees. We need different sorts of woodland. We need to think in terms of wildlife. We have got to start planting on private land – literally, in people's gardens. It's like the IPCC says: we need "rapid, far-reaching and unprecedented changes in all aspects of society".'*

For once, Mary takes a breath. She casts a glance at the window of her office, which is, I realize, identical to my old window when, for a few years, I worked at Swansea University myself. But her bright, incisive manner – all gestures for emphasis and darting eyes inside her heavy-framed glasses – is absent for an instant only.

'The problem is,' she says, 'we all just echo-chamber. The barrier in front of all of this is people. Until I am able to engage with some SUV-driving soccer mom who thinks I'm a hippie who wants her children to be poorer than her, and wants her to eat tofu, we're not going to get anywhere. What we actually need are thousands of communications projects. Really, if it was me running the world – which happily it isn't – I would be focusing entirely on getting across the communication barrier, and the kind of politically motivated reasoning that holds us all back. We are completely stalled until we deal with the fact that only half of the Western world actually wants to do anything about this stuff . . . You know, I talk a lot with women in my climate communication work and when they think no one's listening they're actually more open and honest about what scares them. And what scares them is the idea of climate people, like Greta Thunberg, wanting them not to be able to buy their children nice things. That's a really valid fear. It's a totally valid fear for a mum to have. But until we get past that complete difference in values, we really can't do anything.'

'As a matter of interest,' I ask, after a pause, 'do you consider Covid, as a zoonotic disease, to be part of your area of study?'

'It's an interesting question,' Mary says. 'For me, because I work on trees and forest, the answer is yes. If you look at where zoonoses come from, they come from the fact that communities are being pushed into having to exploit wildlife – from illegal deforestation and the fact that we don't have indigenous peoples being able to use their forested areas to hunt in a sustainable and low-level way. Everything's tied together. Colonialism absolutely decimated tropical forest. It put us on a pathway to viruses jumping between species, probably a hundred years ago. Obviously, zoonoses have always done this. This is nothing new. But it's much worse now. And certainly, when it comes to pandemics, the informed people think they'll be coming thick and fast, from here on out. If we look at it: the pathology and frequency of so many natural-world bugs is getting worse and worse. So, the tree diseases that I work on are worse every year. They're at a higher level, they're spreading more easily, they're affecting more trees and they're becoming more complex. We now don't think of individual pathogens affecting trees, we think of decline syndromes: these multi-faceted syndromes that involve viruses, bacteria, fungus, climate change, everything ... There really is this 360-degree pressure on every single element of the biosphere, and Covid is a part of that. It's another huge problem which exemplifies how broken our relationship with nature is.'

*

The trees continue for three and more hours. Here, the roar of hidden lorries meets the roar of the River Eden; its spray joins the drizzle to soak the rhododendrons, the fern-hung oaks and the leaf-littered ground. Here, near a place called Cefndeuddwr, the trees part for a banking meadow, its moist grass scattered with broad-limbed oaks, patterned with miniature pignut flowers and bluebells bothered by white-bottomed bees. Here, in yet another spruce, a crossbill looks up from his work – plump and red, then instantly gone – while, beneath him, the hardcore and the ruts of machines dissolve into a track of dribbling bed-rock, punctuated by once-laid stones.

'Sarn Helen,' says the map.

The village of Trawsfynydd, as it turns out, is by no means the ungodly place you might suppose as you speed towards Bangor or Holyhead with one eye on the hulking block of its decommissioned nuclear power station. Leaving the A470, you cross a thick-set, three-arched bridge, its river curling to the lake, Llyn Trawsfynydd, between fields pale with dandelion seed. Then you come among tidy terraced houses, their tiny lawns not brutally mown, fringed by wealths of flowering shrubs. The sky is dry and swirls with swifts. A teenage couple appear from a street of more recent, slate-faced houses and set off up the pavement for the Cambrian Garage – she allowing a hand to hang, which he receives without a glance.

Everybody gives their greeting.

At the till in Siop Glyndŵr, a woman of about my age taps up my water and chocolate bars, raises her voice to be understood through her blue face mask and the plastic screen and the mess of Welsh and English we seem to be speaking. The woman has long hair dyed coal-black and glasses like those of Mary Gagen. Originally, she comes from Blaenau Ffestiniog – the best of all towns, in her opinion – and since Sarn Helen passes there as well, she knows several parts of the route.

'Where are you from, then?' she asks.

'Radnorshire,' I say, then, when she looks confused, try the name in Welsh, 'Sir Faesyfed?'

'Oh, Sir Faesyfed!'

On the terrace of the Cross Foxes, a pub with that scoured look more usual on exposed coasts, I sit at one of the picnic tables, sip half a pint of ginger beer and pretend not to listen to my neighbours' conversation. A man and a woman in rude middle age, they are discussing their morning's work, charting the course of an eight-mile run around the shores of Llyn Trawsfynydd.

'How close,' I ask, once we have met through their dog, 'are you able to get to the power station?'

'Very …' The man looks down the narrow street and, for comparison, settles on a nearby shed. 'Ten feet?'

'Really? I'm surprised.'

'Well, I used to work on the nuclear submarines and I was astonished.'

With a blast of Capital FM, the bar door opens and the waitress appears: a bright-cheeked, physical girl in leggings, carrying chips and cutlery.

'They say,' she says, overhearing our talk, 'they're going to tear it down and build some of these micro-reactors.'

'Does it bother you at all,' I ask, 'that it's there?'

'Me? No, not at all – except for that you can't swim in the lake. It's been there all my life, you know. It's just heritage, isn't it?'

On the flank of Mynydd Maentwrog, a couple of miles to the north of Trawsfynydd, is a Roman fort named Tomen-y-Mur. Its views reach further, by some measure, than those of any other fort along Sarn Helen. Scramble through these multiple bogs, through a couple of ditches and on to the motte that the Normans built beside the *principia* – the Roman headquarters – and there is Wales as far south as Cadair Idris: a black impression in the cloud-hung sky. Swallows bank and sweep and plunge. The sheep are faint beneath the A470: the SUVs

towing jet skis and caravans, the troupes of screaming motorbikes. Beside the road are the strip of the village; the huge lake,
dark as the sky and the mountains, cut by a curious system of
islands, like a hieroglyph to be read from space; and the two
squat reactors of the power station, secure at least from sea level
rise – unlike, according to UK government analysis, twelve of
our eighteen other nuclear sites. In the west, through a breach
in the mountains, you can even see across Porthmadog and the
Glaslyn Estuary to a blaze of light: the sea and sky around the
Llŷn Peninsula.

Once, about six years ago, I decided that it would not do,
never to have met Jan Morris – being as she was, by wide con-
sent, the greatest living writer in Wales. I set out for the Llŷn
and for Llanystumdwy, a village I know reasonably well, from
teaching nearby at Tŷ Newydd, the National Writing Centre of
Wales. After wandering among its lanes, I found a house that
seemed correct, having a bust of Admiral Fisher on the garden
wall. I knocked. There was no reply. The woman next door
advised me to wait. The Dwyfor Valley, at the worst of times, is
defined by air and light, by half-hidden bedrock and the sessile
oaks clasped around its torrent of a river. On that August afternoon, it was Wales at its utmost. For forty-five minutes, perhaps
an hour, I sat beneath a brilliant beech, read, watched the birds,
considered a swim; then voices sounded some way off and I went
to look past the neighbouring farmyard at a cavalcade of figures
approaching on a long, straight track. As it transpired, Jan could
not have been more gracious – and particularly once we had
understood that our Welsh was similarly poor. She relished,
it seemed, people coming to pay court. She provided tea and
cake, a thorough tour of her library of a house and talk encom-
passing most of Welsh history. But the scene that remains, the
scene that returns with even a glimpse of the Llŷn Peninsula,

is that initial appearance: Jan, then almost eighty-nine years old, having written all that morning, returning from a walk of hours with Elizabeth, her partner of sixty-six years, in the late-summer sun, with, around and behind them, their multitudes of grandchildren.

Sarn Helen appears now and then on the map, as it makes its way towards Blaenau Ffestiniog. One stretch dives into forestry felled perhaps a couple of years ago: a snare of brambles and climbing roses, which, together with the endless brush, soon have your legs awash with blood. 'Don't worry! Summer's coming!' a man exclaims, his ruby face beaming from a yard full of lorries. The next stretch climbs from the Cynfal Valley, whose knobs and growths of rock protrude out of pockets of sessile oaks, some of them still in the gold of their flowers. A gull turns, white in a leaden sky. A great tit busies in a crab apple tree, shedding showers of pristine blossom. Then the trees are gone, the drizzle resumes and there is only brown and grey: a landscape less despoiled than defiled. In another long, bare field, this one parted by the rushes of a stream, sheep converge from every direction, tripping, colliding with one another – the mothers clamouring for my attention, the lambs clamouring for their mothers.

In these desolate uplands it is as if it is always February, as if even the end of May cannot provide for these wretched animals.

And meanwhile there is this sense of being witness to a very slow explosion. These hills of bogs and cotton grass seem less to pass beneath your feet than to be consumed in turn by the barren rock of the slopes ahead. By the time that you have crossed the ridge above the River Teigl and are inching down the bank towards the overgrown railway, there might be nothing left to the world but slate – whether on the dark, wet roofs of the town or in its girdle of exhausted quarries, its mountains torn to their lifeless cores. On Manod Road I plod through the rain, swapping sides as the pavements require. The Wynnes Arms is boarded up. A few of the windows in either terrace have adhesive tropical scenes – some including the 'Yes Cymru' stickers expressing support for Welsh independence, others praising the NHS.

Just before the turn on to the High Street, a metallic-blue BMW swoops into a space and a man climbs from the driver's seat – all white trainers, tight black jeans and hair directly from the posters in the barber's. Exhaling a menthol fog, he swaggers through the gate of a small grey house and shakes hands with the man waiting on the step, who then slides a small packet into his pocket.

Even so, even after eleven hours' walking, with one foot wet and a way to go before any hope of an accommodating wood, the town of Blaenau Ffestiniog seems a good deal more appealing than it did on my last visit, fifteen years ago. Then, for £30,000, you could pick up a pair of these shops, together with both of the flats upstairs. The takeaways, as I remember, sold nothing much but deep-fried chocolate bars. The town may never recover its slate – its original reason for existence – but this is the May Bank Holiday weekend. Tourists are swarming the aisles of the Co-op, hurrying in cagoules over the rousing phrases set into the pavements round the Information Centre, pouring in and out of restaurants which, if hardly grand, cover most of the bases of Indian, Chinese and Italian food. Here is a gang of local girls, cackling beneath umbrellas. Here are a couple of amorous Poles. Here are a bookshop, a craft shop and a gift shop – and if you would like to own such a premises, according to the window of Tom Parry & Co., it will cost you £85,000.

At the end of the High Street is a rugby pitch, whose posts and floodlights give the angle of the rain. On the fringe of the pitch is a straggle of houses and, cuckoo-like, a monstrous chapel – the street is monochrome apart from one pink gable – and behind them is a mountain of broken slate: a tip so tall, so precipitous you can hardly believe that it stands at all.

It must be like living under a volcano.

II

Maenofferen Slate Quarry to Coed Creigiau

30 May 2021

As you emerge from the deep, mossy wreckage of the buildings in a corner of Maenofferen, their little group of Douglas firs and sycamores whose flowers are teeming with bumblebees, you can see, on the quarry's sheer, bare sides, the former levels of former years. Tracks, half-swallowed by tumbled tips, hang alongside the ghosts of walls. On a ridge stand a gable poised to collapse and the pyramid of a chimney stack, both of them stark in the pristine sky, still, as yet, in the shadow of the mountains. Maenofferen is a hill removed. From these traces you can almost imagine the men who once would have slaved on these slopes and in the then still-covered caverns, loading tramway wagons with slates to be dispatched to the roofs of the world.

Somewhere a cuckoo is calling briskly.

Down in Blaenau Ffestiniog, the sunlight claims another terrace.

Such work as continues at Maenofferen amounts, really, to picking through the rubbish. The ruins where I have passed the night lie just to the north of the quarry's floor, its diggers, crushers, lorries and conveyor belts – all of them still among heaps of broken slate such as you might use on a path or flower bed. Besides employment for perhaps six men, and distraction for whichever children went charging around the milling sheds, hurling stones through the last of the windows, the place would seem to be of little use to anything other than the rhododendrons, which envelop this path with their mangrove limbs, their waxy leaves and fierce-pink petals.

The path climbs at a steady diagonal, gathering a skin of grass and bilberries and then a pair of narrow, twisted rails. Between them is a cable, equally rusty, writhing over the ground and the chunks of shattered slate until suddenly it rises towards the coming sun and a silhouette on the brink of the hilltop: two walls supporting an enormous drum. It is nine feet tall or thereabouts, a thing of cast iron and heavy timber slats with a mechanism like a pair of jaws by way of a brake on its left-hand rim. The drum being on its original axle and still half-wrapped in yards of cable, it is difficult to see inside – though you can make out, in either end, a triangular space about the size of a resourceful boy.

'Your drum, Chris?' I send off a picture.

'It's very very similar,' Chris Meredith replies.

It struck me once, while reading *Mercian Hymns*, the extent to which there is a dream of England. Geoffrey Hill's best-known collection, published in 1971, explores the past and present of his native West Midlands. Its structure is provided by the life of Offa, the late-eighth-century Mercian king who conquered much of central England and, of course, gave his name to the dyke that was to delimit Wales. Hill was no writer of nationalistic verse – his is a 'Coiled entrenched England' – but this remains the story of a conquering people, a people whose preserve it is to define and so to imagine their land – just as it is, in later years, to cross into Wales on 'summer weekends', to drink tea 'by lakesides where all might fancy carillons of real Camelot vibrating through the silent water'.

England was chosen; Wales was not.

If Wales was ever dreamt at all then perhaps it was down there, at Dolwyddelan Castle. To the north of the moor above Blaenau Ffestiniog, its cotton grass and its scintillating pools, the Penamnen Valley opens abruptly. Here, at its arching head, it is all sharp slopes of spruce and streams which course across the naked rock, but at its foot, as deliberate as ever, a section of Sarn Helen follows a river into forestry recently felled. The remaining brush lies in lines like hay. Dolwyddelan, the village, is hidden by a ridge, but its box-like castle is visible, just, like an extrusion of its craggy hill. Its shape is one of the shapes of my mind, along with the likes of Captain Najork, Black Vaughan, Tintin and 'Mae Hen Wlad Fy Nhadau'.

The blues of the mountains grow pale with the distance.

Dolwyddelan Castle stands apart, being a Welsh castle built by the Welsh and therefore part of an exclusive group including, notably, Cricieth, Dolbadarn, Dinefwr and Castell y Bere. It was established by Llywelyn ap Iorwerth – Llywelyn the Great – who was born nearby in 1173, held the throne of Gwynedd from 1195 to 1240 and became in effect the Prince of Wales, though he did not use the title himself. His grandson Llywelyn ap Gruffudd – Llywelyn the Last – had no such qualms. From 1258, as Prince of Gwynedd, he described himself openly as Prince of Wales and, in 1267, even received recognition as such from Henry III of England. It was a short-lived triumph, the last, brief moment in which the country – or most of the country – was governed by a single native ruler. In the 1270s, with the accession of Edward I, crisis after crisis deprived Llywelyn of his lands. By 1282 he was reduced to a fugitive. According to one of the many stories, he passed a final night in a cave above Aberedw, a village not far from where I grew up, before his betrayal to an English knight by one of the villagers.

It is a story that has festered since. Jeff Davies of Court Farm, Aberedw, described to me once how, before the Beeching cuts, passengers departing Aberedw Station would often shout 'Traitors!' from the windows of the carriages – goading the locals into pursuit, into trying to land a blow before the train had gathered speed.

Such national dreams as you do encounter, woven into the writing of Wales, tend rather to be those of pre-Saxon Britain – all Britain, of course, in these versions of history, rightfully belonging to the Welsh. For centuries, the origin myth described in *Historia Brittonum* and, *c.*1136, in Geoffrey of Monmouth's *Historia Regum Britanniae*, was core to any conception of Welshness. The line of British kings, so Geoffrey writes, was born with the arrival of Brutus, the leader of a band of Trojans and great-grandson of Aeneas, who defeated the giants resident in 'Albion' and then renamed the island after himself. It ended with the death of Cadwaladr the Blessed, but its glory is eternal thanks to King Arthur who, together with the wizard Merlin, staved off the Saxons for many years – before at last he was carried to Avalon and the British survivors drained away into the hills and mountains of Wales.

The best attempt I have encountered to develop this story into a dream of Wales itself can be found in *The History of Radnorshire* by the Rev. Jonathan Williams MA. Completed in about 1818, although not published for sixty years, his singular take on Britain's past rejects Geoffrey of Monmouth as fiercely as it does the 'bare and unjustified' accounts of the Roman writers. Instead it opens with the arrival in this island of Huysgwn, leader of the Brixones, a people deriving from the Caucasus whose accomplishments include the invention of the alphabet. Huysgwn names his discovery Albion after the Welsh words *haul* ('sun') and *byw* ('life'), reflecting his people's devotion to the sun. It is a devotion, faced with tireless rain and cloud, that they very soon transfer to fire, changing their island's name to *Bru-Tân* ('Womb-Fire') instead. Theirs is a land of enlightenment, possessed of astonishing technical ability but sworn to the principles of peace and justice. Its inhabitants refuse to erect great fortresses, since to them this would be ignoble – just as it would be to 'circumscribe' God in a cathedral or to compose an epic in the manner of the *Iliad*, thereby privileging fiction over truth. Confronted, as the years elapse, with Romans, Saxons, Goths, Picts and Irish, now and then a Briton is left no choice except to renounce his pacifism. Ninian, naked and single-handed, goes so far as to assault Julius Caesar, belabouring him with his *celt*. But, by and large, the principles hold and the British simply and peaceably retreat.

The result, once again, is Wales: a sanctuary for Huysgwn's vision and emphatically not, 'as some modern wits have inferred', for a people 'spiritless and pusillanimous'.

The trouble is that the Rev. Williams does not stop his story here; the ghost of *cyfran* haunts his pen. North Wales, he finds himself forced to concede, has been corrupted by the Irish influence. And West Wales, of course, is a nest of bandits. In fact, it seems, the only part of Wales that has really upheld Huysgwn's original principles is Radnorshire – and then 'South Radnorians were ... distinguished traitors in former times; some of the present race seem to maintain a tincture of the same mean spirit, and dereliction of patriotism.' In the end, you have to suspect, the only part of Wales to have maintained the national vision is the very small part of North Radnorshire containing the Rev. Jonathan Williams MA.

St Elen's Well, in Dolwyddelan, occupies a bank rich with blue-bells and buttercups. Over the past four hours or so, the sky has blossomed into small, high clouds but the sunshine, mostly, remains uninterrupted; it falls full into the square of a pool whose walls are ferns and yellow primroses, herb robert and foxgloves yet to flower. The A470 roars behind the trees. In one of the uphill corners of the pool, near where the spring trickles over the leaves, a rock is used by visitors to crouch and pray or wish or drink. I set down my rucksack, hat and sunglasses. I lower myself from the wall to the rock, then slip and suddenly immerse one boot – scattering the water-boatmen, turning the well into a storm of silt.

Maybe twenty years ago, when my brother was living in St Petersburg, he and I went travelling in Siberia. After a week or two, we arrived in Tuva: one of the 'autonomous' Russian republics, straddling the boundary of *taiga* and steppe. Like its neighbour Mongolia, Tuva is majority Yellow Hat Buddhist, though the religion overlies a shamanist tradition which, in many parts, remains in health. Once we reached the forest around Lake Azas, Russia seemed almost a memory. There was the mesmeric overtone singing of the Tuvans. There were the depthless stars at night. Above all, there were the *arzhaans*. Wherever we went, by bus or truck, everyone would stop every handful of miles at yet another of these sacred springs, to add to their offerings of stones or sweets, to tie another rag to the neighbouring trees. Perhaps it was the mood of our Tuvan companions, perhaps it was some quality innate to the place, but to visit, to drink at an *arzhaan* seemed always to bring a sense of clarity, a strangely heightened sense of attention. Soon enough they came to seem a natural fact. That the landscape contained these points of focus – these 'places through which everything passes', as they were explained to us – had needed only to be pointed out. Obviously, it seemed to me, you could read any landscape on earth in very much this way.

Water, Professor Austin said, as he paced the ruins of Strata Florida, is sacred universally. Springs – these sites where water passes from the darkness into the daylight – have been 'spiritual centres', *axes mundi*, over tracts of time beyond all reckoning. Two thousand years ago, tradition suggests, the Roman legionaries would stop here at St Elen's Well as they marched between Caer Llugwy and Tomen-y-Mur to quench their thirst, to pay their respects. But this is only one of the hundreds of sacred springs known to exist in Wales. In *The Holy Wells of Wales*, Francis Jones names 1,179: 1,179 places through which, perhaps, everything passes.

Both archaeology and written records give abundant evidence of the ancient significance of holy springs and wells. Jones cites seventy-six Welsh examples with megaliths or tumuli built nearby, in apparent recognition of their sacred character. In *De Excidio et Conquestu Britanniae*, Gildas, the sixth-century monk, rails against 'the blind people [who] paid divine honour' to 'fountains'. Wells were worshipped, it appears, as, or as the abodes of, gods; they were considered liminal, portals where such powers as the Otherworld possessed might be brought under human control. That such traditions required contortions of the early medieval Church is plainer again. Despite the views of the likes of Gildas, in AD 601 Pope Gregory I advised

Augustine's mission to convert the 'temples' of the English 'from the worship of devils to the service of the true God; that the nation . . . may the more familiarly resort to the places to which they are accustomed'. The poet Taliesin embodies this confusion: the fact that the coming of Christianity to Britain was no more a clean exchange of faiths than has been the coming of Buddhism to Tuva. In the Taliesin poem 'An Unfriendly Crowd', the poet writes both *'Lauda tu, laudate Jesum'* ('One and all, praise Jesus') and 'The *awen* [inspiration] of my song/ I draw up from the depths' – by implication, from the Otherworld.

Across Wales, the Christian Church co-opted the sacred springs, assuming control of their purported powers. The names of some may predate Christianity – those, say, with the names of trees, birds or animals, especially such outliers as Ffynnon y Fuwch Frech, near Llansannan in Conwy, the 'Freckled Cow' being a stalwart of Welsh folklore – but most have the names of saints or other aspects of Christian practice. Churches and chapels have been built at or near them: almost 200 altogether. In the *Lives* of the saints, springs erupt at every opportunity – in recognition of prayers or miracles, to mark the spot where a saint's tears fall or a saint's staff strikes the ground. They appear spontaneously at the baptisms of both David and Catwg; the latter, though a baby, leaps into his, dipping himself three times in honour of the Trinity. And when, after a thousand years, the Church resumed its struggles with springs – they were condemned by the Protestants for their Catholic association – many of these formerly holy sites simply evolved into 'wishing wells' or else reasserted a medicinal function, becoming destinations in the name of science. St Elen's Well is said to be good for sickly children and paralysed limbs. Others claim benefits for asthma, blindness, rheumatism, scurvy, fractures, toothache, cancer, melancholy, ague, nasal pains, hair loss, warts and every other affliction you can imagine.

Nor are these places – even the most obscure of them – necessarily forgotten. Professor Austin described with relish the discovery by a colleague, in 1999, of a holy well high above Strata Florida. Noticing, in an aerial photograph, a mysterious space in a forestry plantation, Caroline Earwood fought through the spruces and came to a well of neatly laid stones bearing a mugful of fresh-picked flowers.

On the brim of St Elen's Well, I drain my boot, wring out my sock and, over minutes, watch the water settle. As its appearance of rage subsides, the coins scattered across its floor return to visibility. The spring keeps trickling. A cloud hides the sun. With a few words of apology, first in English, then in Welsh, I lower myself again on to the rock and wait and pay my best attention. Whatever the reason, for me at least, here is the calm, the rootedness that these places always possess – even in the absence of garrulous Tuvans. I close my eyes and cup my hands and, as I trouble the surface of the pool, so the sun returns and bands of light come trembling across my face.

On a good day in late May, even the most homesick of Roman soldiers must have given himself to Caer Llugwy. The sides of its valley are dense with oaks, their underwood hazel just as it ought to be, their floor dead leaves and moss-fattened rocks and bluebells vanishing into the shadows. The floor of the valley has oaks of its own, though mostly they cede the level ground to the sheep and instead clamber over its humps and hillocks, ringed by hawthorns in brilliant flower. Visitors continue to discover its charms. Facing the fields where the fort once stood, across the stony, duck-paddling river in its honour guard of sycamore and ash trees, there is a campsite and walking centre. Bell tents shine among camper vans. A couple of families are playing a game of cricket. And here in the lane, doubled up, motionless, is a man of distinctly urban appearance – his trousers and T-shirt the grey-blue of the tarmac, his black hair cropped but for a spike at the forehead.

Hovering nearby with mountain bikes, a young couple make awkward gestures: a woman in Lycra and a little mascara, a man in shorts and a ginger beard. They peer from beneath their gleaming helmets at the man balled up like a hedgehog at their feet. Neither is sure what they should do. He has, they say, acknowledged their presence but nothing more than that. He has, they suspect, taken ketamine, though they lack the conviction of personal experience. The pressing risk, clearly, is that of cars; the man is remarkably camouflaged, with the oaks hanging dark above him and his face largely buried in his chest.

The Good Samaritan, we all agree, would never have forsaken the traveller, even if the traveller was in a k-hole.

Suddenly, the man falls sideways. He is older and bulkier than I had realized. Now he is blocking the lane entirely, his head hanging into the central chippings with eyes clenched shut and tears of sweat running freely over his cheeks. Then, with a long and wrenching roar, he vomits a noxious yellow-brown sheet. He vomits again, and then again – the force enough to thrust him backwards, so that he ends up, groaning quietly, in the bluebells strung along the verge.

The immediate danger, it seems, is past.

The couple and I pool our resources and leave behind a bottle half-full of water.

*

'There's a huge conversation,' says Jennifer Rudd, 'going on in Welsh government. They're trying to think strategically about where we can spend a lot of money to make a huge cut in our

emissions. *They're trying to take the holistic approach, to think: OK, how do we bring agriculture and public sector and businesses together? Whereas the Westminster government has gone, well, we'll just have a tech fix. They've gone for carbon capture and storage, as if carbon capture and storage will fix everything. And it's ... just not there yet!'*

The potential for negative emissions technologies (NETs) – removing greenhouse gases from the atmosphere – is something that Dr Rudd understands. As well as being a climate change educator and a Senior Lecturer at Swansea University, she is a specialist in carbon capture and storage, climate change mitigation and the circular economy.

We are talking on Zoom in September 2021.

'OK,' I ask, 'so could you give me an impression of where NETs are at and where they're likely to go?'

'This will help.' Jennifer revolves on her chair, digs in the drawer of a filing cabinet and brandishes a heavy report. 'Greenhouse Gas Removal. It's a couple of years old but it's the Royal Society and the Royal Academy of Engineering. So ... It says, "In the UK, reducing greenhouse gas emissions to the greatest degree considered feasible would leave around 130 megatonnes of CO_2 per annum by 2050. Offsetting these emissions with greenhouse gas removal to reach 'net-zero' for the UK is possible, but very challenging. It involves deployment of many different greenhouse gas removal methods, and import of biomass ..."' She gives an empty laugh. 'So, we need a "ramp-up of forestation, habitat restoration and soil carbon sequestration now, research and development of currently unproven but promising greenhouse gas removal methods and establishment of substantial infrastructure and capacity for carbon capture and storage" ... so even the darn report admits that the tech isn't ready yet!'

'Can we start with carbon capture and storage, then? Where are things with that?'

'Well, there are different tech fixes there. One is that you burn biomass. This is something Drax [Power Station] say that they're doing. This is carbon that has been captured already, by the trees, so if you burn it then all you're doing is emitting already-captured carbon, and you can call it carbon-neutral. And if you can capture that carbon dioxide, you could call it carbon-negative. Drax is trialling this, and I think they're capturing about a tonne of CO2 a day. The major issue I have with it is that they're importing a lot – a lot – of their biomass. It's coming from America and Canada, which obviously has huge embedded emissions in the transport. And we know we need to be planting more trees, so how does that fit?'

'A tonne of CO2 a day,' I ask. 'What does that mean in terms of our current emissions? I mean, to put it in some sort of context?'

Jennifer turns to her calculator, frowns into her long, narrow glasses. 'If you take the global greenhouse gas emissions for 2017 – that's about fifty-four gigatonnes of CO2 equivalents – and divide it by 365 . . .' She punches in the numbers. 'Then you get 0.15 gigatonnes per day.'

'That's . . . 150 million tonnes per day. So one tonne is not really –'

'Anything . . .' She gives that laugh again. 'And do you want to know the kicker? They then release it!'

'What?'

'They literally just release it! I've battered them on Twitter about this, and they say, "It's only a demonstration." At least find a freaking greenhouse to dump the stuff in!'

'OK,' I say, 'so . . . biomass is difficult. What about other technologies?'

'Another type is to do with heavy industrial emissions,' says Jennifer. 'So, if you think about Tata Steel down in Swansea, or the cement factories. Or think about Hull and the Humber, or

Teesside – *you know, they've got huge emissions, but they're also close to disused oil fields or disused gas sites. The plan there is to capture those industrial emissions off the top of the stacks and to compress the captured carbon and push it back out under the North Sea along the pipelines, and then seal it up. There's loads of geologists who have worked on this, and they are happy that they could seal the carbon dioxide back under the sea where the methane originally came from. The pipelines are there. The infrastructure's there . . . For Swansea, they're looking at shipping it round to Ireland to then dump it – again, in a controlled way, I don't mean just chuck it overboard . . .*

'*The problem is, the capture is really challenging, because even though you're looking at maybe 20 per cent CO_2 coming out of the stack, or even higher concentrations – and that's great – a load of other nasties come out at the same time. And it'll be really hot, and have water vapour in it. So you need to create a capture material that wants to grab your carbon dioxide, that can cope in wet, that can cope in humidity, that can cope in heat. And you want to be able to create it at a low cost because we've got to make loads of this stuff. And you've got to make sure it has a low embedded carbon footprint because otherwise what's the point? You've also got to be able to cycle it round and round, so it can capture, release, capture, release, time and time and time again: you need a reversible reaction, otherwise you've got to throw the whole lot away, and generally that reversal involves heat or pressure. At the moment people are using liquid amines – carbon and nitrogen together – but there's a 30 per cent energy penalty for using those materials . . . So, while there are places that can do it, there aren't many of them and they're expensive to run. The better thing would be to use solid capture materials, but they're not really there yet, and they're certainly not scalable.*'

'But I'm right in thinking, am I,' I ask, 'that these technologies are likely to be more effective than direct air capture?'

'Ye-es . . .' says Jennifer. 'Well. Potentially, yes, because you can put them on top of stacks and you've got a concentrated flow of CO_2. Direct air capture's really interesting because, in theory, you can just put it anywhere and it'll capture CO_2 out of the air. The problem you've got is that carbon dioxide only accounts for 0.04 per cent of the air, so you need something that's really, really, really selective. And again you need a reversible reaction. What Climeworks were doing was putting it on a building then using the waste heat from the building to provide the thermal capacity, the 100 degrees needed to remove the CO_2 from the capture material. At their test bed in Switzerland, they were then pumping the CO_2 into a local agricultural greenhouse and food was growing about 20 per cent larger because it was in a higher CO_2 concentration, and now they're putting it into fizzy drinks.'

'You mean, they're not getting rid of it either?'

'Well, what they then did was they partnered with Iceland – Iceland the country, not Iceland the food store. And because they've got geothermal, you're getting the free heat to regenerate the capture material, but they're also then piping it down, getting it to react with the calcium oxide to create calcium carbonate. They thought initially that the process would take a decade or something, but because of the elevated temperatures down there it was only taking 400 days. They were basically turning it into chalk. And now they've unleashed . . . Orca they call it: this big capture plant. It cost about US$15 million. But all that it's capturing is 4,000 tonnes a year – about 870 cars' worth of emissions. I mean, it's huge, it's groundbreaking, and . . . it's doing almost nothing.

'I'm not going to lie, I am disillusioned with carbon capture and storage. When I first heard that we could hit 4°C of global warming, I just wanted to shut everything down, turn everything off. As I've understood more of the policy angles and the business angles, I'm less inclined to say we should do that, but I want to see action now – and, honestly, I would throw carbon capture and storage out of the mix, because I think it's a distraction. I think Westminster's using it to say that will fix it, so we don't have to make the hard decisions – and we should be making the hard decisions.'

'By which you mean things like ... ending the steel industry?'

'When I say hard decisions, I mean things like behavioural change, like putting a carbon tax in place, like really going after the private sectors and the big industries, and getting people to count their carbon emissions and make a proper plan for reducing them. I mean not building new coal mines, not expanding airports, not allowing more petrol cars, not allowing more gas boilers. I think those hard decisions mean aggressively pursuing the things we can implement right now, that are ready ...'

'But,' I say, 'from what you've said, you must know those things are not going to cut it? Even if you look at, say, farming in Wales. Look at the advice of the CCC [Climate Change Committee] in sum and that's all but an end to the livestock industry, within a generation. That's revolutionary, in itself. And even that time-frame is reliant on the UK being able to capture and store – what did that report say? – 130 million tonnes of carbon dioxide every year by 2050. If we throw out carbon capture and storage, then surely all those things really do have to stop right now. Right? I'm sorry ... I don't mean to bring you down ...'

The expression on Jennifer's face is desperate. Even with the distance of Zoom, there are obviously tears in her eyes, and although she is a climate scientist, although she must live with this information all day, every day, I feel appalling – sick, in fact – for having caused them.

'It's really hard,' she says, eventually. 'I can't cope with it. I just can't cope with it ... Or, rather, the only way I can cope is to act. I have to go to bed at the end of every day and say, have I done something that means I can live with myself, that means I have tried to protect the world for my son, and that I have raised awareness of climate change? So, I'm running a climate change education project. I've moved from engineering to management in order to try and effect real change, right now. Am I living the lowest carbon lifestyle that I can get away with, you know, without making my husband really miserable? And still enjoying life? And if I can answer those questions then, well, that's what I can do ...

'Though I honestly believe,' she says, a few moments later, 'we are having more and better conversations than we were two, three, four years ago. When I did a speech in front of the Science Museum the other day, one of the things I said was that I've worked on climate mitigation technology for years, but most of that time I thought fossil fuels were running out – that that's why we were creating solar panels, that's why we were creating a hydrogen economy ... How was it that, eight years post-PhD, in a climate change-related field, having gone to a university with a Green Campus and a Green Chemistry department, I still didn't know where we were heading? How is that even possible? It was only when I got to Swansea, only when I sat down with a couple of guys – they were working through these various scenarios of what happens at 1.5°C, what happens at 2°C, what happens at 4°C – and I went, "Heck, we're not going to hit 2° of global warming, are we?" And they said, "We're going to hit 4." And ... everybody I have conversations with – and I do try not to sit in my bubble – they do know about climate change now. They know they have to do something.'

She hesitates, then looks away, her left hand held to her chin and her throat.

'Can I ask you, then,' I ask, 'what you think most needs to be said?'

'These are the main things for me,' she says, turning back to face me. 'We've got to figure out how to communicate with people and understand how we activate them. That is key. And we can't just think that it's schoolchildren we need to activate. It is too late for that. We need to educate the entire population, and we need people to understand that the scientists aren't going to come in and fix this. We need every sector of the population – you know, people who are really thinking through where our clothes come from, people who are passionate about divesting pension funds. We need sociologists and psychologists to understand human behaviour, we need lawyers to make sure we get environmental law enshrined, we need economists to look at a new model ... I think this is the problem we've got. Everybody's now aware of climate change. There's a general awareness that you should turn off the tap, and turn down your heating, and you shouldn't go away and fly on holiday, but not a lot of people have realized that everybody has their part to play in the wider solutions. Everybody needs to look at their job and look at their life and go: how do I leverage my skills, my talents and my resources to battle climate change? And we've got to believe that we can do it, because if we don't then we might as well not bother. We might as well all go to Australia on an aeroplane and drive a six-litre SUV. If we don't believe that we can do this, then it isn't going to happen.'

*

Swimming back across Llyn Bodgynydd, there is nothing to hear but my circling limbs, another cuckoo hidden in the woods, a family on a distant bank, laughing over their fishing rods. With the afternoon, the clouds have gone; the sky is a richness undepleted even at the summit of Carnedd Llywelyn, even in the spires of the firs. An island is crowds of willows and birches. The water is cool, clear, coloured with peat; its surface is a landscape of blue and black. Nailed to a trunk by the shallow cliff where I pull myself back into the air a sign reads 'CCTV Is in Operation', but no boughs part to reveal a telescreen. Nothing interferes with the year, come into its weightless height.

The path feeds on, skirts fallen trees and upswelling rock in the forestry. It joins a lane, its verges strewn with glittering camper vans. It crosses a slowly climbing field where big lambs, seeking the security of milk, hoist up the hind parts of their mothers. The mountains scatter in sculptural splendour, away into the south and west – cradling lakes of silver-blue and trees, some deciduous, most coniferous, stretched and draped like the shadows of clouds.

Then the field folds; the mountains are gone.

Half a mile distant is Llanrhychwyn Church. And there, above its hunkered roof, above the hedge-knit Conwy Valley, is a deep-blue triangle: a wedge of sea.

Recently, on a Sunday morning, I cycled the eighteen miles down the Usk Valley to St Edmund's Church, Crickhowell. Although Christianity continues to elude me, this was a designated 'Climate Change Service'; I felt that I should know what was said. So I sat on a pew in the centre of the nave, socially distanced like all the congregation, and stood on instruction and bowed for the prayers and grew no fonder of tambourines and considered Christ upon his cloud among the intersecting tracery of the big east window. I listened and I felt, more acutely than ever, the terrible hollow at the heart of our culture where once, for many or most of us, there would have been God. It is this hollow, I suppose, that draws me back and back to the *llannau* – finding, as I do, a peace in their stillness, in their wonder, their exultation. Whether or not there is a universal answer, the need is real and God at least is sustainable – unlike hate, or alcohol, or perpetual acquisition. And with God, as well, come conceptual structures that permit some understanding of the climate emergency: structures exceeding our individual interests, structures our secular culture so desperately lacks.

As the Reverend Khan intoned:

> Creator God, maker of heaven and earth,
> we acknowledge our failure to live responsibly
> as part of your creation.
> We have taken what we want,
> without considering the consequences;
> we have wasted and discarded
> without thought for the future.
>
> Open our hearts and minds to the signs of our times,
> to the groaning of creation,
> so that we may turn from our greed and lack of vision
> and see
> a world being made anew in Jesus Christ Our
> Lord. Amen

Llanrhychwyn Church, a sign suggests, is the oldest surviving church in Wales. With the exception of the sixteenth-century extension, it is hard to know what could have changed since the early thirteenth century, when Llywelyn the Great worshipped here, together with his wife Siwan, Lady of Wales. Under a roof of hand-cut slates, the walls are low and fatten towards the foot – you have to push the door up and away – and, once inside, there is very little more. There is a pair of parallel naves, divided by heavy-set, whitewashed pillars as well as a few right-angle pews. There is, at the head of the older, south nave, a small table by way of an altar, its window depicting in honeyed golds a Trinity of peaceful, inquiring faces. There is no heating. There are no lights besides the candles on the altar and the candelabra hanging from the ribs of the roof.

The font is square, a millennium old – among the first to succeed the river baptisms.

The only sound is a nearby cuckoo.

It is where Celtic Christianity departs from its inspirations – from the likes of St Anthony of Egypt – that it reveals its difference: its enduring, underlying culture. We see what is when we see what it's not. Barricaded in his derelict fort, Anthony can seem, above all other things, to be in mortal struggle with his physical self. His body is 'corrupt', as Athanasius writes. His 'bodily necessities' are a source of shame so vehemently to be controlled, to be shunned, that he will sometimes eat as little as one meal of bread and salt every four days. As with the bestial in himself, so with the bestial in the world. Once, in an almost touching moment, 'the wild beasts of the desert' injure his crops. 'But he, gently laying hold of one of them, said to them all, "Why do you hurt me, when I hurt none of you? Depart, and in the name of the Lord come not near this spot." And from that time forward, as though fearful of his command, they no more came near the place.'

This is a man in the model of Adam: a man with 'dominion ... over all the earth'.

It is a model that holds, to some extent, for the Celtic saints as well. Both in Welsh and Irish tradition, the living world is there to serve: a curlew saves Beuno's sermon book as it is falling into the sea; stags offer their services to everyone from Brynach to Illtyd, Teilo to Finnian of Clonard; a fox carries a psalter between the young Ciarán of Clonmacnoise and his master in his cell, while the air itself carries their conversation. And yet 'dominion' is not quite right. In Celtic Christianity, there is the shape of a richer relationship with the natural world. The curlew rather helps than subjects itself to Beuno, very much as a bird drops a feather when Laisrén of Devenish decides to write a book. The sense is one of willing, of reciprocation. The fox's devotion to Ciarán is returned when, in flight from a pack of hounds, it hides itself beneath his cowl. The stag's devotion to Illtyd begins when, so as to escape King Meirchiaun the Mad, it takes refuge in the saint's bedchamber. And when Melangell, the Irish saint who found her seclusion in Montgomeryshire, shelters a hare in the folds of her robes, she does so purely out of compassion. Perhaps, then, this is the better word: a common, a universal compassion – like that of Kevin of Glendalough who, while praying in a cell so small that one arm has to protrude from the window, suffers a blackbird to nest in that hand, to hatch and to fledge her young.

Unlike the Romans, the Celts of Wales did not have an urban focus. Both before and after the occupation, most of them lived rurally, as part of an extended family unit gathered together in a hamlet or hill fort. Their traditional religion was, naturally, animist: that is, a system of belief which reverences all living things and often attributes a spirit to such non-living things as springs and rocks. 'For,' explains the Rev. G. Hartwell Jones in the 1912 edition of *Y Cymmrodor*, 'the savage extends to the universe his own implicit consciousness, and regards all natural operations as intelligent beings, gods or goddesses, of forest and field'. Animism has been denounced throughout Christian history – or at least dismissed, as Hartwell Jones has it, as typical of 'the less progressive classes'. Nonetheless, it was from this ground that Christianity grew.

These were the structures that guided the saints, that guided St Rhychwyn, if the legends are correct, to found his church in

this exact place. It is a place befitting the afternoon, for all the
detritus piled beside the churchyard: a chain harrow, a one-
wheeled trailer, a Land Rover with an elder sprouting in the
cab. A blackbird flutes in one of the yew trees. To either side,
above the churchyard wall, the arms of the hill reach high and
wooded; they frame the fields which fall away through flowering
hawthorns to that verdant valley, that sunlit sea. It is a place to
transport, to transform. Its church, as T. J. Hughes would surely
observe, has no need for a spire or tower, for an architecture to
guide your eyes towards some other, ethereal heaven. Rather,
like a holy well, like an *arzhaan*, the building marks a point in
the landscape possessed of an inherent power, an intensification,
perhaps, of the force that the saints called God. As with the
stories of the saints, with their stags, their foxes, mice, wrens,
curlews and badgers, you need only look to see in Llanryhchwyn
a reverence for the animating principle as it is revealed in the
natural world.

12

City of London Magistrates' Court

22 April 2021

*I would like first to thank the court for its time and for this oppor-
tunity to speak.*

*My name, under regular circumstances, is Tom. I am forty-five
years old: a writer and a tutor in Creative Writing. I have two
parents of retirement age. I have two children of primary-school
age. I am a member of Extinction Rebellion . . .*

Courtroom 2 is cool and quiet. In its grey fitted carpet, in its
discreet light, in its panelled walls and its veneer desks, it has
the atmosphere almost of a library. Besides my voice, so far as I
can tell, the only sound is the air-conditioning – though London
must be contained in that hum, as an undertow, an obscured
roar. To the back sit Sharon, an XR volunteer, and my old and
estimable friend James Miller. The court itself, since I have no
solicitor, comprises only a couple of clerks, the prosecutor – a
young white man with a grey-blue suit, strawberry-blond hair

and a day or so's stubble – and the magistrates, both white men of advanced years, their bench, with its Perspex screens, elevated by two or three feet, roughly to the height of the dock, where I stand.

This is the other reason why it is not until May that, finally, I will return to Sarn Helen – to the last few dozen miles between Dolgellau and Caerhun. Although the climate and ecological emergency often seems to be my only thought, it has taken every spare moment for weeks to resolve which of its strands to discuss, how to stitch them into this statement.

My son Edwyn is eleven years old. Edwyn is a kind, sharp, long-limbed boy, athletic in a way that I never have been, taller than I was at his age. In the mornings, Edwyn likes to get up before me, to creep downstairs and hide to make me jump when I come for my tea. This amuses him endlessly. After this, in the spring and the summer, the two of us will often go and walk in the lanes and test one another on the flowers in the hedgerows. Edwyn likes to fight me, and Edwyn likes to hug me. He worries. He likes things orderly. At the moment, he is fascinated by the folk guitarist Richard Thompson – although, these past few weeks, he has also become interested in evolution, especially the famous story of the peppered moth, and in Welsh history, especially the circumstances around the death of Llywelyn ap Gruffudd.

His sister, Alice, is eight years old. There are times when I think that I am exaggerating when I say that Alice never stops singing, but this is more or less the case. Unlike Edwyn, Alice does not like the mornings, but you know when she wakes up because the singing starts: a slightly husky voice, rich with vibrato, powerful enough to be heard throughout the house. She makes up her own songs, as she always has, and her songs are beautiful, perfectly pitched. Until the pandemic closed it down, the children's mother, my partner Charlie, ran a café in Brecon, our local town. Outside the café there is a sill, where Alice would install herself and, with a Tupperware pot at her side, perform her songs for passers-by. She could sometimes earn more than £10 in an hour. Alice is small and dark in complexion, with hair that reaches past her waist. She is fiery, imaginative, often stroppy, very ticklish, very keen on cuddling and very, very sociable. When her hair is tied in a bun, she resembles Little My from the Moomin *stories.*

In the mornings, normally, we will cycle down to school. On the long, narrow lane called Warren Road, Alice will lead, I will ride in the middle and Edwyn will come at the rear. When we reach the busy roundabout at the bottom of the hill, I will go first, with Alice in the middle and Edwyn at the rear, and lead them into Llanfaes, to their school. We resemble, I often think, a duck with ducklings. I do this because these are the best configurations to make sure that they are safe. In the evenings, after their supper, I will invariably read to them. I have read them everything from The Lord of the Rings *to* Grimms' Fairy Tales, His Dark Materials *to* Cakes in Space. *I do this because we all enjoy it, and because it settles them down in peace and in security. I do these sorts of things all the time, because I am an ordinary parent, because I love them beyond words and it is my duty – my absolute responsibility – to look after them.*

For the second time since I began this statement, I find tears pushing into my eyes and am obliged to stop and breathe. It is a disconcerting experience, being on trial when you have never so much as seen a courtroom before. (My previous arrest, in 2019, did not lead to a charge.) It is, paradoxically, deeply familiar: entirely like being returned to a classroom, with the standing-up when the magistrates enter, and the addressing of the magistrates as 'sir', and this sense of being summoned to the teacher's desk to give a lengthy reply to a question. It is familiar, too, in ways that I could never have expected. For one thing, there is the chair of the magistrates, with his soft, warm voice and his foliate tie, with the glasses he requires to see any distance, with his short white hair and his short white beard. It is not just, let's be honest, that he seems like a man who might easily be a friend of my parents. As the prosecutor was connecting the television on which the witness and the evidence would appear, the chair informed me of his love of Wales and that he often goes riding in the Black Mountains – hiring his horse, as we quickly established, from some good friends of mine. 'It's a small world,' he observed. And at the same time, compounded by the sense of school, this whole affair has the cast of a dream. It is unreal, to me at least, that a case like this should ever be brought. It was unreal, as we all watched the bodycam footage of my arrest in Parliament Square, to hear again the riot of the drums, to see myself sitting there in the road, in this same jacket and this same shirt, bent, as if braced in resistance: me in a group with Jay and Henry and, as I had failed to clock at the time, and as if this was not unreal enough, the actor Mark Rylance.

My worry is that the magistrates will take my tears as a symptom of this disconcertion – not, as they are, of the horror of what I need to say:

In 2050, Alice will be thirty-eight and Edwyn forty-one – close to the age I am now. On current trends, we will long have exceeded the IPCC's 'safe' upper limit of 1.5°C. We will have reached 2°C and, according to recent analysis from the Institute for Economics and Peace, impacts compounded by this heating will have displaced 1.2 billion people from their homes. 1.2 billion people: children, women and men, people like ourselves.

By 2070, when Alice will be fifty-eight and Edwyn sixty-one, we will very likely have reached 3°C. A study, published in the American Proceedings of the National Academy of Sciences, *suggests that 3°C will leave about a third of the world's population living in 'extreme heat': conditions, at present, extremely rare outside the hottest regions of the Sahara Desert. One of the lead authors of the study, Professor Marten Scheffer of Wageningen University, has described such conditions as 'unliveable'. Another study, published last year in the journal* Nature Communications, *suggests that, by 2070, the Amazon rainforest ecosystem – home to more than 3 million species – may well have collapsed and become instead 'a savannah-type ecosystem with a mixture of trees and grass'.*

'There will,' Professor Scheffer has said, 'be more change in the next fifty years than in the past 6,000 years.'

By 2080, Alice will be sixty-eight and Edwyn seventy-one. They will be approaching the current age of my parents. By 2080, under what the government's Climate Change Committee (the CCC) calls the 'business-as-usual trajectory', there is every chance that we will have reached 'the extreme danger threshold of 4°C'. To quote Professor Steven Sherwood of the University of New South Wales: '4°C would likely be catastrophic rather than simply dangerous. For example, it would make life difficult, if not impossible, in much of the tropics, and would guarantee the eventual melting of the Greenland ice sheet and some of the Antarctic ice sheet', which could see a sea level rise of several metres.

For 2100, when, maybe, my children will be eighty-eight

*and ninety-one years old – younger, still, than my grandfather
is today – multiple models, including those of the UN World
Meteorological Organization, the Canadian Centre for Climate
Modelling and Analysis and the American National Center for
Atmospheric Research, suggest a possible, unimaginable 5°C.*

And, of course, neither time nor heating will stop there.

*To quote Professor Stefan Rahmstorf, of the Potsdam Institute
for Climate Impact Research: 'Like in the Covid pandemic, timing
is critical to prevent devastation. If you wait until you already
have a serious problem, then it is too late.'*

*To quote Sir David Attenborough, speaking two years ago this
month: 'It may sound frightening, but the scientific evidence is
that if we have not taken dramatic action within the next decade,
we could face irreversible damage to the natural world and the
collapse of our societies.'*

*To quote Lord Nicholas Stern, I. G. Patel Professor of Economics
and Government and Chair of the Grantham Research Institute
on Climate Change and the Environment at the London School
of Economics: 'Climate change is the result of the greatest market
failure the world has seen. We risk damages on a scale larger than
the two world wars of the last century. What we are talking about
is extended world war.'*

*This, on our current course, is the future that we are leaving
to Alice and Edwyn – and to your children, and to yours, and to
yours.*

The magistrates sit with their heads at an angle. Their faces give
nothing but professional attention.

I wait again, and then resume:

I was, I think, brought up well by my parents. Thanks to them I am, I think, a good, a moral person. You will note, I hope, that I have never before been charged with any crime.

The climate crisis, the scientific basis of which is endorsed by 98 per cent of all publishing scientists – a consensus greater even than that around evolution – this is not a natural disaster. This is not an earthquake or a meteorite strike. The IPCC has existed for thirty-two years. Lyndon Johnson, as US President, was briefed on the science of global heating as far back as 1965, and the heating effects of atmospheric carbon dioxide and methane were well established long before that. We – collectively – have known the consequences of our actions for decades, and we have continued regardless.

This means that, through our behaviour, we are consciously inflicting the impacts I have described, or else assuring the strong likelihood of those impacts, on ourselves, on our children, and on billions of other people: impacts including thirst, hunger, displacement, injury and death. Following the definition in my Oxford English Dictionary, *this is, to me, quite clearly a crime – 'an evil or injurious act; an offence, a sin; esp. of a grave character' – and a crime on a scale unprecedented in human history.*

If I am a moral person, I cannot simply observe this crime. I cannot simply be complicit.

What, then, am I to do? Well. Like thousands upon thousands of others, I have signed petitions and attended protests and, if only once, organized a protest myself. As a writer and as a campaigner, I have written and spoken publicly about climate and ecology on more occasions than I can hope to remember. I have travelled village halls giving talks. I have written and spoken to local councillors, and written and spoken to my Member of the Senedd, and written and spoken to one MP and to another MP ... And for all of those who have done the same and very, very much more, despite fifty years of such fine organizations as Greenpeace and Friends of the Earth, fundamentally nothing has changed.

Our government has not listened.

It has failed even on its own terms. In 2019, by the assessment of the CCC, it missed twenty-four out of twenty-five of its climate targets. As Lord Deben, the chair of the CCC, said at the time: 'The whole thing is run by the government like a Dad's Army. We can't possibly go on with this ramshackle system; it doesn't begin to face the issues. It is a real threat to the population.' And since then there has been no improvement. Of the thirty-one milestones for actions recommended to the government by the CCC for 2020, for example, only two were fully achieved.

In March this year, the Public Accounts Committee concluded that the government has, quote, 'no plan' for addressing climate change.

Given which, it might be reasonable to wonder how it was that, in May 2019, the UK Parliament came to declare 'an environment and climate emergency' – the first such declaration by any parliament in the world – and that, in June 2019, the UK government signed into law a target of net-zero greenhouse gas emissions by 2050, which, at the time, was the most ambitious target of any major economy.

What brought about this sudden change? Well. As regards the climate emergency, here I quote Jeremy Corbyn, the then leader of the opposition, as he moved that motion on 1 May 2019: 'We are witnessing an unprecedented upsurge of climate activism with groups like Extinction Rebellion forcing the politicians in this building to listen … Today we have the opportunity to say: "We hear you."'

'"We hear you."'

As regards Theresa May signing into law a target of net-zero greenhouse gas emissions by 2050, here I quote the House of

Commons Library, Acting on climate change: The plan for net zero emissions in the UK: *'In 2019, following Parliament's declaration of a "climate emergency" and recommendations from the independent Committee on Climate Change (CCC), the Government legislated for net zero greenhouse gas emissions.'*

I hardly feel I need to labour this point. Where petitions, and protests, and talks, and meetings with politicians have failed, the tactics of civil disobedience used by Extinction Rebellion have been, to some measure at least, successful. As well as resulting in unprecedented levels of public concern about climate change, the actions of April 2019, in which I am proud to have participated, if too briefly, led directly and demonstrably to Parliament's declaration of a climate emergency, with the 2050 target 'following' from that decision.

Manifestly, this is cause and effect.

The reason why I am here today is that, on 1 September last year, I sat on the road in Parliament Square for approximately one hour, holding a piece of paper reading 'Support the CEE Bill' – that is, the Climate and Ecological Emergency Bill tabled in the House of Commons by the Green MP Caroline Lucas – and did not cooperate when asked to move by a police officer, PC Andrew Dixon, whom I would, incidentally, like to thank for carrying out his duties with civility and professionalism.

In this act, I would like to emphasize, I damaged or injured nothing and nobody.

To those I inconvenienced, I apologize sincerely . . .

I do not want to become a criminal. I do not deserve to become a criminal. I can state, without the ghost of a doubt, that to do as I and thousands of other members of Extinction Rebellion have done was not merely justified, it was an absolute moral obligation.

I would, in conclusion, like to mention the custody officer who, on the night of 1 September, locked me in a cell in Charing Cross

Police Station, where I remained until midday on 3 September. He was a little younger than me perhaps, softly spoken, a wearer of glasses – though, as my own glasses had been taken at the desk, I missed the details of his appearance. This officer, having brought me blankets, food and water, returned to the corridor and went to close the door, but then stopped and said to me:

'On behalf of myself and my children, I want to thank you for what you have done.'

I ask the court, please, before it comes to its decision, to reflect on that officer's words.

Thank you again for your time.

Outside the tall, gold-curtained windows spaced along the wall behind the magistrates, the plane trees of Bucklersbury remain in bud. It is easy for me to see the great, bright windows and the sandstone slabs of the Bloomberg Building. The magistrates would have only to lean to look across Queen Victoria Street to the steel and marble of HSBC, the second-largest financier of fossil fuels in Europe. If you accept, in so far as this is possible, the consequences of our use of fossil fuels and of our devastation of the natural world, then, necessarily, you live with a dissonance: you accept that to participate in our society is also to participate in its destruction – through flying and driving and heating your home, through purchasing food and purchasing clothes, through making tea and mowing your lawn and browsing the internet and building an extension and writing a book and almost any other normal activity. This dissonance, however, can rarely be so acute as it is in the face of the legal system: these people who implement the rules by which normality is maintained. Since this trial began, two hours ago now, there has really been no question that I will be found guilty. As the chair of the magistrates will soon explain, not one of my lines of defence can be considered within their 'narrow' terms of reference. But the unyielding reality of the experience is a different matter again.

The magistrates are one thing. There are magistrates, as there are judges, who have chosen to acquit in cases of this sort; they have allowed themselves to exceed the prescribed terms, to look to justice in a wider sense. That these magistrates do not follow suit is scarcely to be remarked upon; this is normality, after all. True, they do not take a moral stand. They make no mention of the substance of my statement. They do not express, in language or manner, any sense of regret at an inevitable decision, but neither, at any point, do they suggest that I committed any wrong. In the end, they are amoral, passive. They facilitate, as somebody must in any historic crime.

The police, in the form of the Assistant Commissioner who authorized the conditions for arrest in Parliament Square in September 2020, are subtly distinct. In the earlier parts of the trial, the Assistant Commissioner appeared as a witness, a face on the television, delivering her statement in the tones of somebody now on the thirtieth time of having to perform this duty. In concluding a survey of XR's history, she observed that 'splinter groups from Extinction Rebellion have engaged in high-profile criminality away from these major events. In September 2019, "Heathrow Pause" planned to fly drones in the vicinity of Heathrow Airport with a view to causing maximum disruption to it. In summer 2020, "Beyond Politics" engaged in a linked series of criminal damage to charities and political organizations' premises which resulted in thousands of pounds worth of damage. The group have indicated they intend to continue to damage government buildings in early September 2020.' Needless to say, these remarks had no relevance to me or to anyone else arrested that day in Parliament Square. We were not committing criminal damage. We were not attempting to disrupt an airport. They were included by the Assistant Commissioner purely to provide a justification for her actions: that is, for dispersing a peaceful protest almost as soon as it began. In this regard, her behaviour was entirely in line with that of the Home Secretary, Priti Patel, who has defended XR's inclusion on a list of 'extreme ideologies' and has publicly considered its classification as an organized crime group. There, again, the intention was to demonize, to smear by association, to scare and so to suppress, and as a tactic, of course, it has had success. It puts doubts in the minds of activists, raising fears as to how they are perceived by other people in their community. It lets the conversation concern the nature, not the message, of the protests. Soon enough it fulfils itself, allowing the climate movement, for better or worse, to be dominated by those who would employ more disruptive methods.

In February 2020, a psychologist friend, David Jones, and I gave a talk in a bookshop in Crickhowell, seeking support for local XR groups. In the usual way, we explained the basic science and then the reasons for XR's approach. There were perhaps fifty people in the audience and, as we drew to a close, a man in the front row who had until then sat mute rose to his feet and asked who would join him in setting up a Crickhowell group. Twenty or more people signed up at once. As these evenings go, it was quite the success. Then, two days later, the news reached Brecon of anti-XR protests outside these people's houses – the argument being, by all accounts, that they did not want 'terrorists' in their town.

Which spelt the end of XR Crickhowell.

To stifle the climate conversation is *actively* to seek global catastrophe.

The fable of the boiling frog, as it was told by our parents to me and my brother, came with a couple of qualifications. The first was that it was not true: the frog would, in fact, hop out of the pan. The second was that a much better metaphor for the human inability to resist gradual but calamitous change was the ewe with her head in a fence. This was a condition that we could understand. Sheep were forever yearning for that verge of a lane or for that flowery fringe of a hay field, and would shove their heads between the strands of wire and graze as far as their shoulders would allow. They were also forever getting into a tangle – of wool and wire or thorns or brambles – and often that tangle would become too much and they would decline into weary passivity, and sometimes, if nobody came along, you would find their skeletons still in that position. The funny thing being, as our father would remark, that if somebody did come along then the fear was almost always sufficient to force the ewe to free herself – however depleted she might have become.

It is only in terms of human psychology that this scene makes any sense.

After a trial of nearly three hours, yet another climate activist emerges from the City of London Magistrates' Court, poorer by £772 (plus the travel and the tie). He passes under the Cross of St George and its motto, *Domine Nos Dirige* – 'Lord Guide Us' – to arrive in Queen Victoria Street and digest the fact that he is now a criminal. Charlie has done it. Jay has done it. This afternoon it is my turn. Later today it will be somebody else: in fact, a man who will be more confrontational, superglue himself to the dock and attempt to livestream the ensuing chaos. Perhaps his approach will prove more effective. Probably these tactics of civil disobedience will be superseded soon enough, as government policy, the escalating crisis and one or other desperate individual spawn their first explosion or large-scale act of sabotage. James and I stand by the spike-topped railings at the mouth of the steps to the Underground station, watching the cars creep round the Bank of England. For these moments, at least, the situation is clear. Nobody is coming along. This is humanity's perfect problem. We are travelling unchecked towards disaster, led by lying governments – and it is neither a help nor a consolation to know that our children will curse them to hell.

13

Coed Creigiau to Caerhun

31 May 2021

As Coed Creigiau gives way to Coed Gwydyr – the two woods are distinct only on the map – the valley behind the layers of leaves looks very much like the Wye Valley as it opens, as its river starts to meander, between Llyswen and Hay-on-Wye. There are no uplands, or none that I can see; on that eastern side at least, the hedge-bound fields just shrink and tilt and vanish into the clean blue sky. Down on the alluvial plain, with its marshy grass and pinstriped crops, a train dopplers south towards Betws-y-Coed, Dolwyddelan and Blaenau Ffestiniog. The sun, still low, glances off the River Conwy, which otherwise is hardly to be seen. The woods run for miles along this bank, their tracks strewn with willow down, the soft-coin seeds of the wych elms, the leaves where the squirrels have been at work.

It is only at the dingle of the River Ddu, a mesh of spiny undergrowth, that you have no choice but to drop to the road whose periodic vehicles are muffled by the trees. There is a path here in theory – on the map, a green dashed line leads to the village of Dolgarrog – but in practice there seem to be only nettles. Then, suddenly, there is an open slope, steep and wet and vivid with bluebells and very obviously a private garden.

On one of several pools of grass, a man turns off his clamorous mower. Silver-haired, in a brown-check shirt, he offers up a brusque 'Good morning,' watches my slithering, halting descent from a wealth of rockeries, weeping trees and marvellous shrubs, their flowers pink with scarlet hearts and white with elements of gold.

'Slept in the woods, did you?' he asks.

'I was staying down near Trefriw,' I say, noncommittally, coming to a halt on his drive.

'That's where you've walked from, then?'

The man is proving hard to read. His stance is oddly puppet-like – his hips tipped the one way, his head tipped the other – and it is only when an eyebrow overtops his glasses that I understand that he is amused. It is barely eight o'clock on the late-May bank holiday; he is in no hurry and my awkward appearance is a good enough reason to procrastinate. So I explain about Sarn Helen, about having walked from Neath, albeit in stretches, about having only three miles left to go.

The crescent of a smile shows in one of his cheeks.

'I'm a Roman myself,' he says. 'Actually, I've been thinking of bringing a lawsuit, to reclaim my ancestral territory.'

The man's name, it transpires, is Giovanni; he is the owner of the Conwy Valley Maze, the largest garden maze in the world – composed of 2,500 yews, most of which he planted himself. There are, he says, a number of Italians scattered around the Conwy Valley. Just over the hill is the Allegri family: descendants of two brothers, POWs who decided to remain here after the war and who married, to regional consternation, two of the most beautiful girls in North Wales. He tips his head to the other side, regards my relatively dark complexion and asks if I might be Italian myself.

'Alas,' I say, 'I had a DNA test. Several bits but none of them that.'

'Everyone ought to have a DNA test,' Giovanni says, 'then wear the results as a badge on their chests. That would stop nationalism dead in its tracks.'

A little way on, in the village itself, the woods loom over agreeable houses of conservatories and flowering fruit trees. Among them is Adventure Parc Snowdonia: a gulf of concrete, steel and water promising, of all things, 'Adrenaline Indoors'. Its Hilton Garden Inn resembles *khrushchyovka*, the prefabricated apartment blocks which litter the former Soviet Union. Its surfing lake is grim as a water treatment works. Across the road, between a children's playground and a run of buildings comprising a craft shop, a café and a hairdresser's, two small signs offer Wall's ice cream and a selection of hot drinks by Nestlé. The village shop, Siop Porthllwyd, is open for business – its one small room crammed with more magazines, more confectionery and postal equipment than there is space for customers.

The woman at the counter brews my tea, keeping the steam away from her spectacles, moving with that particular formality characteristic of village hall fêtes.

'Covid,' she says. 'It does make you want to do things you haven't done, doesn't it?'

'Has it made you do anything?' I ask.

'Just be grateful for the things we've got, really.' She glances at the double-glazed window, past the hotel and the lake to the hills, their radiant fields daubed with the shadows of the hedgerows and the woods. 'It's a beautiful place we live in, isn't it? It's easy to forget that sometimes.'

The village of Castell is a last stretch of cottages, of small, bright cars on tarmac drives, hanging baskets, shrill-voiced dogs. It dwindles into a last stretch of road, winding with the easy, valley-bottom contours so that you have to swap sides only now and then. In a lay-by, a lorry is asleep between Polish number plates, next to a cemetery awash with flowers wild and sown and left on graves.

On the right is an ivy-covered gateway.

You see St Mary's Church, Caerhun, across a broad field: a gleaming roof among a few tubby yews, perched on the brink of the riverbank – the River Conwy sheer in its bed of mud. St Mary's is unusual, if not unique, in Wales in being built on a Roman ruin. There is a church on the site of the fortress in Caerleon and another in Caerwent, apparently assembled from the stones of the Roman town. In Holyhead, the Roman fort was given to St Cybi by Maelgwn Gwynedd, the sixth-century king, as Gildas has him, 'soaked in the wine of the Sodomitical grape'. Perhaps much the same thing happened here. Perhaps some forgotten local prince bestowed Canovium Fort on some forgotten local saint. Or perhaps the saint simply adopted the place, in emulation of Anthony of Egypt.

Here the lane parts a lip in the grass; it would have been the south-west angle tower.

Here a sycamore marks the house of the commandant – once, so archaeologists suggest, a fine building of red Cheshire sandstone – while a second sycamore, a fat lamb in its shade, stands in the *principia* whose plastered walls were patterned with leaves and red and yellow stripes.

Ditching my rucksack in the churchyard's shaggy grass, its plantain and forget-me-nots, I try the door beneath the church's double bellcote, its single bell like a winking eye. It is locked, says a sign, because of Covid-19. Above me the gable is backlit, speckled with sandstone. The eaves of orderly, elderly slates are raucous with house martins, swarming, chasing over the headstones of George Scragg and Ceinwen Hext, Mary Nickson and David Price, Robert Roberts and Agnes Dain, Charlotte Williams and Jessie Shaw and Major Robin Glen Burness Watts. Some of these are remembered in English; others are remembered in Welsh. Like the church, the wall of the churchyard appears to have been built of salvaged Roman stone – perhaps by the same Cistercian monks in the thirteenth century. It is not high. You can see across the ramparts and a stretch of tawny reeds into a vale like a mirror of Neath, its wooded hills gathering into the south, where the sky holds a few grey-footed clouds.

It is still not ten o'clock. There is nobody here, nobody in sight – or only the glint of the A470, there in the trees on the far side of the valley. And so I heave myself over the wall, hop a fence, dodge a clutch of nettles and saunter past the site of the garrison bathhouse, past a few willows in a light-filled line. The River Conwy glimmers, ebbing, branching around the long, rippled shapes of its shoals. You can just taste the salt in the exposed mud, a sharpness deep in its decomposition. By all accounts the river is not currently navigable – it has silted up, towards Tal-y-Cafn – although, as the IPCC has explained, regardless of anything we might now do, 'sea level will continue to rise for centuries'. The models for RCP8.5 see this valley as a limb of the ocean stretching south all the way to Trefriw – just down the hill from Llanrhychwyn Church. One more willow tops a finger of ground, jutting to the water in a run of little stones, which is all that remains of the Roman docks. To the churring of the traffic on the road, to the mirrored light playing in the brim of my hat, I sit, take a breath, eat a bag of nuts.

Here, 1,900 years ago, the Roman galleys would ride the tides to land or collect their supplies and men.

Here it was that Sarn Helen ended and the rest of the world began.

Epilogue

Caerhun to Great Orme's Head

31 May 2021

Over the Conwy's trio of bridges, along with the railway and the A457, a causeway carries a manner of park: bushes, flower beds, lawns and paths where people stroll in the vertical light. Often they pause to photograph themselves, framed by the hulk of Conwy Castle, its vast barrel towers patrolled by children, or else by the yachts on their buoys in the harbour – turned with the tide towards the powder-blue sea. You can hardly hear the plaints of the gulls for the voices high with this blessed convergence of sunshine, holiday and lockdown done. Some are English. Others are Urdu, Polish, Hebrew, Yoruba. One of the paths steers north with the shore, around a tranche of weed-smeared mud. Now a man in yachting shoes, their mouths revealing miniature socks, hauls in his inquiring spaniel. Now a woman swings a sequined purse, her chest and shoulders coloured to the shape of the vest that she was wearing yesterday. The air is one of gathering prosperity. Deganwy Marina is the home of the gin palace: such fat craft as the *Lady Windsor*, with its white-leather seats and its pristine decks and its elongated tinted windows. The houses here are opulent new-builds, honey-gold and temperate-grey, each with a car in a personalized number plate: Range Rovers and BMWs, even a McLaren F-1.

Llandudno, as the Welsh press seems often to remember, is a desirable place to live. Turn the shoulder of Marine Crescent, where the estuary funnels and jet skis fight the flow; leave the last of these wide-eyed villas, their palms and occasional castellations; join the path around the North Wales Golf Course ('Beware Golfers' one sign reads) and there, across the bay, across West Shore Beach, its bats and balls and children digging to Australia, you are looking at the full Great Orme: a limestone headland two miles long, serpent-like as the name may suggest, cut with barren, sinuous strata. There, a little apart from the town, is a line of very large, tree-masked houses, their very large gardens tended to the water, which comprise the most expensive street in Wales.

Even for a street not defined by its consumption, you might think Llys Helig Drive a name provoking fate. On the map, Llys Helig is a natural reef not far off the coast of Penmaenmawr with a separate feature just to its south in the shape of an extended W – apparently a fish weir of great antiquity, still seen at very low tides as recently as the nineteenth century. In legend, though, it was the court of Helig ap Glannawg, father of St Rhychwyn and Prince of Tyno Helig: a land which lay to the north of Wales until, one night, it was swallowed by the sea. It is not just that Llys Helig Drive is at risk of flooding – although, even as things stand, many of its houses are exposed. According to the models, a storm surge on a high tide, with a rise in sea level of 1.5 metres, would leave most of Llandudno under water. The Great Orme, in fact, would become an island. And according to the IPCC, for all the uncertainty surrounding timescales of centuries and millennia, the long-range forecasts for RCP8.5 suggest a 'multi-metre (2.3–5.4m) rise'.

It is none of it hard to imagine, looking down across the gorse and the buttercups on the southern slopes of the Great Orme. Llandudno lies on its neck of land with barely so much as a single contour. As the sea closed in from the north and west, first it would overtop the Parade and enter those magnificent Victorian hotels; it would send an arm down Abbey Road and another into Queen's Road, reaching for the Co-op. Then it would consolidate, sever Gloddaeth Avenue, settle down three streets from the Front – purging the takeaways, the chartered accountants, the beauticians and the osteopaths. Then the change would be swift, extreme, perhaps resulting from the sort of storm that, in 1917, finished off the village of Hallsands in Devon, if on an entirely different scale. The cricket and football pitches would be drowned, along with John Bright Comprehensive School, along with businesses in multitudes – Asda and Aldi, McDonald's and Costa – along with the better part of the town's houses.

It is harder to imagine how this could be stopped. Llandudno, a town whose whole appeal is its beaches, would need to be surrounded by defences. And then, peering back towards the hazy impressions of the Snowdonian hills and mountains, there are just so many other priorities. There are the million-pound houses of Deganwy Quay. There are the low-lying mouths of the Conwy Tunnel. There are the Holyhead railway and the North Wales Expressway – both of which, in every scenario, face inundation all along this coast.

As for Cardiff, 130 miles south, it might have the Cardiff Bay Barrage to provide some protection from the sea. But the low-lying land to its north and south means that this could easily be circumvented. One paper published in 2020 puts the Welsh

capital at number six of eighty-five world cities at risk from the
effects of climate change – the sole reason being sea level rise.

At the top of the slope is Ty'n-y-Coed Road, tucked in a
wooded fold of the headland: unprepossessing pebble-dash
houses and cottages with red-brick chimneys, climbing flowers
and neat, terraced gardens. With the angles of the streets and the
strata, with the weight of the sun on my head and my shoulders,
for a moment everything appears askew – even, there, across the
terracotta roofs, Llandudno Bay with its scribble of surf and a
speedboat sketching out figures on its blue.

Cable cars pass through the few cirrus clouds, heading for the
town or the summit of the headland.

Llandudno ends in St Beuno's Road.

St Martin of Tours, the man who, more than any other,
directly inspired the Age of Saints, spent much of his time
resisting the devil – at least, so his (contemporary) *Life* suggests. His greatest challenge, by some measure, comes when
the devil appears to him in the guise of Christ 'come down
upon the earth'. For 'a long time', the saint is simply 'staggered'.
Living, like so much of the fourth-century Church, in daily
expectation of Apocalypse, for once he is almost persuaded; he
almost believes that this is indeed Christ, returned to reign for
a thousand years.

Strange and remote as St Martin might seem to us, we are,
of course, heirs to that same tradition, creatures of that same
culture. Activists attempting to raise awareness of the climate
and ecological emergency are endlessly charged with 'doom-
ism' – with claiming that catastrophe can no longer be averted.
And often enough, it has to be said, these charges are fair
enough. Imminent societal and ecological collapse are spectres
of the climate movement. Our culture contains its established
paths and, given our failure to address climate change, the path

marked 'apocalypse' can seem the only choice. It is familiar. It has that comfort. And besides, catastrophe is already here – in Bangladesh and Washington State, Ethiopia and New South Wales. And besides, the obvious alternative – the equally well-worn path, 'salvation' – is really not a path at all. The scientists 'aren't going to come in and fix this', as Jennifer Rudd said.

Not least because the climate and ecological emergency is not, in the end, a scientific problem. Science might provide the tools to understand its nature, to model and to mitigate, but the emergency is a symptom, it is not a cause. The cause is us: our deluded conviction that we can live in isolation from the rest of the world.

It is three o'clock in the afternoon: three hours until the last of the trains that could see me home before the end of the day. For all the miserable condition of my feet, and of a knee now hardly willing to function, it feels wrong not to walk to the cliffs, to stop and consider the world to the north. A track creeps past a well, Ffynnon Powel, across a bank of brilliant gorse to terminate in a loop of lane, the small, unremarkable Church of St Tudno and a churchyard where a family with Liverpool accents are wandering on thin, pale legs. Another family – they appear to be Afghan – park their Audi to pose for some photographs. There is a bench in the narrow shadow against the church's plain north wall. It looks over graves and a dazzling hawthorn, down a plummeting slope to a peaceable sea, its blueness streaked with lateral currents, punctuated, towards the horizon, by hundreds and hundreds of wind turbines: pure white figures in military ranks, wading towards Ireland like King Bendigeidfran.

St Tudno, so history suggests, washed up on the Great Orme in the sixth century. He founded this church to mark the spot – the town, Llandudno, inherited its name – though he seems himself to have lived in a cave on the almost inaccessible tip of the headland. As for Tudno's provenance, you might suppose that he came from the North: Cumbria, Strathclyde, the Isle of Man. North Wales owes a good deal to these places; historically, they have formed a cultural sphere very much like South Wales, Devon and Cornwall. Legend, though, points in the opposite direction. Tudno is said to have adopted the life of a monk in recompense for the sins of his father, Seithenyn, the notorious drunkard, who failed to close the sluices of Cantre'r Gwaelod and so condemned that entire land to vanish under Cardigan Bay.

The thing about the Age of Saints is that this was the beginning of Wales. It was then that the Brittonic language evolved into Early Welsh. It was then that a border was imposed by the Mercians, pagans, whereas in Wales the very pattern of settlement became obedient to Christianity. That was the beginning. This, now, may be the end. Certainly, under multiple scenarios, Wales as a distinct entity could very easily cease to be – with the collapse of our agricultural communities, with the inundation of our coastal towns, cities and infrastructure, with inland flooding, with the scourge of zoonoses, with the impacts deriving from the Global South and other countries rendered uninhabitable, with our devastation of the ecosystems on which we rely.

It is not to submit to apocalypticism to acknowledge that the world will very far exceed the 'safe' upper limit of 1.5°C – that, in our collective inaction, we have already chosen for our children a future of deep uncertainty. It is not to deny human ingenuity to recognize that scientists will not be our salvation. The question is no longer if the crisis will happen. The question is how bad the crisis will be. This is the fight that we now face. It is the fight of our lives, in which everything matters: every fraction of a degree, every species we save from extinction, every person who will not just watch, who finds the courage to find their role.

At stake is all that we know and love.

The fact is that our future depends on a transformation without peacetime precedent: a reinvention of our society and economy around completely different principles. Some, in the West, have looked elsewhere for these principles, often in indigenous cultures. Myself, I would suggest that if they are to endure then they cannot only be imported, any more than they can be conjured from the air. As with Christianity in the Age of Saints, or with Cistercianism in the Middle Ages, they cannot hope to take root in our culture unless, to some measure, they already belong. In Wales, this is where we might remember the saints. Look to the foundation of this country, and you see the likes of St Melangell, facing down the hounds of Brochwel Ysgithrog – purely to protect the quivering hare hiding underneath her cloak. You see the likes of St Illtyd, in the Hodnant Valley – a stag, by his own volition, drawing timber to build the saint's church. You see the likes of St Tudno and St Rhychwyn, refugees from flooded lands, each siting his church in praise of the Creation, each bearing witness to an ancient culture led by a reverence for the natural world.

For the natural world to be the first consideration is not, in fact, and despite all appearances, alien to the culture of Wales.

Indeed, it is its very heart.

Acknowledgements

Many, many thanks to everyone who has lent their time and thoughts to this book: Chris Blake, Jenny Bullough, Will Bullough, Gerwyn Davies, Jeff Davies, Claire Earlie, Marie Ekström, Jay Griffiths, Robert Hughes, Andy King, Gwyn Lewis, May Lewis, Toby Litt, Ruth Lloyd, Victoria Lloyd, Christopher Meredith, James Miller, Marlene Mutter, Matthew Price, Walter Price, Cliff Pugh, John Pugh, Paul Roberts, Jennifer Rudd, Paul Sinnadurai, Judith Thornton, Aaron Thierry, Robert Tyler and Charlotte Ward.

Many, many thanks as well to Clare Alexander and Laura Barber. You are wonders both.

To Linden Lawson, Christine Lo, Pru Rowlandson and all at Granta.

And to Jackie Morris. You have made my year.

I am also hugely grateful for financial help from the Literature Wales Writer's Bursary supported by The National Lottery through the Arts Council of Wales and from the Authors' Foundation grant from the Society of Authors.

Finally, I would like to thank Christopher Meredith again – both for the permission to quote from 'Borderland' (*Air Histories,* 2013) and for the image I use to describe him at Maen Llia. The original can be found in 'John Blight at The Land's End' in his superb *Still* (2021).

With love as ever to Edwyn and Alice.